D1525020

17 REASONS WHY BUSINESSES FAIL

Unscrew Yourself From Business Failure

Pooja Agnihotri

Acknowledgments

I am deeply grateful to my brother, Neeraj Agnihotri who motivated me to write this book and who read my early drafts and shared his valuable suggestions. Not just that, he even designed my book cover. Without his assistance, this book wouldn't have existed.

Writing this book was a great challenge to me as I tried to balance so many other projects at the same time. And none of this would have been possible without my life partner and my loving husband, Todd Perelmuter. Turning an idea into a book is as tough as it sounds and if not because of his constant love and support, this idea would have remained an idea.

I am forever indebted to my parents for their trust in my abilities and for helping me become the person I am today.

A very special thanks to the team of Bizadmark. They worked extra hard on every project which gave me some time on my hands to finish my book on time.

Lastly, I want to thank each and every person who always believed in me.

INTRODUCTION

Dreams remain dreams until we decide to act upon them. We're never too young or too old to make those dreams come true.

When we finally make up our mind to start our business, we are doing more than just bringing our vision to life. We are fighting against every odd, every ridicule, every criticism, every stereotype and every negative thought that has been directed in our direction just because the others were not able to see what dreamers like us did.

That business could be the first black owned publishing company in Chicago or the first female owned bookstore in Baltimore. That business can even be a theatre run by an LGBTQ person, a grocery store run by a seventy-year-old army veteran, a cafe run by a young and single mother, or a tech company run by an immigrant.

To get back to my point, whatever kind of business you own, I know it was not easy to start it in the first place. It would have taken a lot of courage, sacrifices, perseverance and hard work. The courage to fight back when people said you can't do it. The sacrifices you've made by giving a part of your life to your business rather than to your family. The perseverance of never accepting defeat and continuing moving despite every fall. The hard work of keeping everything under control irrespective of the baggage on your shoulders.

Maybe now you're finding it too hard to continue carrying that baggage. Maybe now you are getting tired of telling everyone that your idea is actually good. It's time to get up on your feet one more time, dust yourself off and prove others that you've dreamed something good and it is worth fighting for. Therefore, the purpose of this book is to prepare you for one more try.

I myself have experienced many failures in my life. I have started at least ten businesses before starting Bizadmark, a successful marketing and advertising agency based in Brooklyn. The success didn't come so easily as it never does. The path was paved with the failures of many other businesses of mine. While walking on that path, I've lost many hours of my life. But when I look back, I only see business lessons. Those lessons I'd wished I knew earlier which are lessons I'm going to share with you in this book.

When I'd started Bizadmark, I worked with a lot of businesses-in-distress. That is exactly what I call them - businesses-in-distress. I had the chance to work with businesses from every domain. From hospitality, education, ecommerce, media, entertainment, technology, healthcare, beauty, fashion, non-profits to artists. The problems were similar irrespective of the industry or business type and most of the mistakes they were making were similar to what I've made a long time ago.

I have worked with over one hundred businesses and artists which most of them were able to bounce back to growth while many others were able to successfully direct their business to a more profitable line. One thing I believe in is that knowledge increases when you share. So, here I am sharing all my knowledge on why businesses fail on the pages of this book.
I hope this book will pave a new path for your business and your entrepreneurial dreams. **Starting a business is not as complicated as you may think, but keeping it running is.**

Why Read This Book?

"There is only one thing that makes a dream impossible to achieve: the fear of failure." – Paulo Coelho

If you're wondering why you should read this book, I will say it's better to learn from other people's mistakes than to do it yourself. As mistakes in a business are proven to be costly and disheartening, avoiding them should be in every business owner's priority list.

Shame!
Embarrassment!
Guilt!
Fear!
Sadness!

These are just a few of the emotions that a business owner goes through when the business starts going down. A phase comes when you start second-guessing everything like maybe I was not supposed to invest money there. Maybe I was not supposed to cut the marketing budget. But now it's too late to go back and fix those problems.

Experts advise that when your business fails, you should take some time off to analyze what went wrong and be brutally honest to yourself at that time. I say why wait until it's too late. If you're aware of what you're doing wrong now, you can fix that problem on time. Also, many times we are not able to hit the nail on the head. What happens in that case is that we start a new business and repeat the same mistakes, hurting the chances of success even for the new business.

That's why I highly recommend you read this book and be brutally honest with yourself regarding the condition of your business right now. This book mainly talks about seventeen reasons that lead to business failure. Once you learn how to tackle those obstacles, you will not have to worry about business failure.

How to Extract Information from This Book

You're going to find a lot of information in the coming pages. If you try to grasp everything at the same time, you will find it hard to remember and apply when needed. The best way to get the most out of this book is to read one chapter at a time.

Once you finish a chapter, take a break and think about how your business is performing in that area. At this stage, you can even invite others from your team to join you in a brainstorming session about what you've just read. If the majority thinks that there is a scope for improvement, then make a plan of action and implement it. Don't forget to monitor it.

After that, move on to the second chapter and repeat the process. Once finished, I will say that you should read this book once a year, so you're guaranteed to never make those mistakes.

It's time to get up, stand tall and start working on your business 2.0. Every dream begins with a dreamer. You're a dreamer and let this book be your guiding tool.

CHAPTER 1

Not Open to Being Wrong

"But the thought of being a lunatic did not greatly trouble him; the horror was that he might also be wrong." — *George Orwell, 1984*

Story of Being Wrong

Once 20th Century Fox studio executive Darryl Zanuck said that the television won't be able to hold on to any market it captures after the first six months. People will soon get tired of staring at a plywood box every night." Let's imagine if he would have not been willing to accept that he was wrong and would have clung to his wrong ideas even more than before. What would have been the future of 20th Century Fox Studio?

In another story, the president of the Michigan Savings Bank advised Henry Ford's lawyer not to invest in the Ford Motor Company because as per him "The horse is here to stay but the automobile is only a novelty — a fad." Henry Ford's lawyer bought the socks against the advice, became a millionaire with the help of those stocks and quit his law practice. [1]

These are just a few examples to show you that anyone can be wrong, even the ones who have been a part of the same industry for many years like Darryl Zanuck. Next time if you feel like saying that the others are wrong because they don't have as much experience in the industry or possess the skills you have, remember Mr. Zanuck. It's very possible that your inexperienced intern knows more than you think, even if you have been part of the industry for over thirty years.

It's okay to be wrong but it's not okay to not accept it. When we fail to acknowledge and admit that we were wrong, we hinder our mind from learning something new.

However, people get easily carried away in their quest for being right all the time rather than being able to put their ego aside and see the whole picture.

This is something that we very commonly see on social media where being right seems like the coolest thing. Let's not forget that most of the arguments that happen on social media are not based on facts but are merely formed on the foundation of guesses, assumptions and opinions. Shutting someone down with sarcasm can make you a temporary hero on Facebook, but you can't run a business with that attitude.

Curiosity Killed the Cat but Saved the Business

Oscar Wilde once said, "Whatever is popular is wrong."
It is very common to get influenced by social media influencers and motivational speakers that trigger unrealistic dreams. It's highly advisable not to become a victim of the Dunning–Kruger effect which is a kind of a cognitive bias which makes people falsely overestimate their skills or knowledge.

As we don't want to be wrong, so many times we pretend to be more skilled and knowledgeable than we are by not accepting we are wrong when we clearly are. When a motivational speaker says you can do it, although it is good to believe you can do it but look at every angle before you do that. You can cross a river by swimming but it's good to learn how to swim before you jump in the river.

People's ignorance is often times invisible to them.
I could have started this book with a motivational speech that you all can build your dream business, but this is an incomplete as well as a misleading statement. There are many layers to this statement which come in the form of your current skill set versus what is required for the business, your current savings versus how much you need to fund your business, and a lot more.

It's wonderful to dream big but you still have to be realistic. If I say I want to start a space exploration business next year, I am not being honest with myself. I know a business like that will need a lot of investment, an understanding of that industry, ability to employ great scientists and unfortunately, I don't have any of those assets at the moment. I can let my ego inflate by arguing with you that I can do it, but ego has never driven anyone to success.

Follow Your Dreams, I Am Living Proof

Haven't we all heard something similar at least once in our lives. This is half true. Let's say you want to be a tooth fairy in Brooklyn in 2021 and want to start making lots of money, how much relevance does a statement like, "Follow your dreams, I am living proof," hold in this case?

No matter how much you want to be, how passionate you're about a field or how many people have told you to follow your dreams, not every field will bring you success or pay you millions. If you still want to be a tooth fairy, go ahead, but keep your expectations straight.

You're Wrong!

"The fastest way to succeed is to double your failure rate."
  -IBM's Thomas Watson Sr.

You're wrong! Even the thought of that is unnerving. Nobody wants that. Nobody likes to be wrong. Suddenly your mind starts to make excuses like, I have twenty years of experience in the beauty industry. Or I have studied from the best university in the world, I have more expertise in this field, the other guy is way too inexperienced to understand the intricacies of this business, my industry is very different from hers, there is nothing she can tell me. Or they are just customers, they have no clue how this business is run.

These are the kinds of thoughts that cloud our mind when somebody tries to tell us something that goes against what we believe in.

Imagine being proven wrong by a thirteen-year-old. You will find it hard to accept their argument because you will think that they have no experience and knowledge to qualify to give you any kind of suggestion. But this is where we lose as a business owner as we let our egos win. To put it differently, when we stick to our views and aren't even willing to consider what others have to say, we lose an opportunity to grow and become better.

One time, William Preece from British Post Office said that, "The Americans have a need for the telephone, but we do not. We have plenty of messenger boys." What would the future look like had the British not opted for telephone as a means of communication their growth would have been badly dwarfed.

You need to have firm determination but a flexible mind if you want to grow.

Without that, you will be controlled by your restricted thoughts.

Restricted Thoughts

Not being open to listen to others and consider what they

are saying can be relevant as well as lead to restricted thoughts. Restricted thoughts will keep you under the illusion that whatever you're thinking is right and anyone who doesn't think the same as you has no clue about how to run your business.

Further, when you say no, you're saying no to new learning, opportunity to increase your knowledge and grow your business. That thirteen-year-old might not know how to run your business, but in spite of that would still be able to show you a new way of looking at the same problem.

You never know where your next big idea will come from. It can come from your marketing team and it can even come from an unknown teenager you just met in a cafe. So, the next time somebody says something about your field, pause and think if there is any weight to that statement.

The Other Side of Restricted Thoughts and Limited Beliefs

Imagine if we were not open to others' views, we would still be living on a flat earth (although according to many, we still are.) We definitely wouldn't have reached where we are now.

Not willing to be open, restricts our belief system. The reason why there are so many issues in the world is because people have restricted thoughts. These kinds of thoughts arise from the stubbornness of always wanting to be right.

The Journey from Close-Mindedness to Open-Mindedness

Once you decide that you're going to make your business successful, you become open to being wrong because you become hungry for ideas. You become interested in figuring out new ways of solving the same problem and understanding different points of views.

It takes hard work to become open-minded. If you're ready to grow, here are a few things that you can do:

- ## Be Ready to Change

  As simple as these words seem, they are pretty tough to implement. Many business owners ignore ideas that come from their junior employee or from their customers. However, I will say that you are lucky that people are telling you what can be improved in your business. You're receiving free ideas.

  It doesn't mean that you have to implement every suggestion somebody makes, it just means that you are going to consider that suggestion and will see how feasible, realistic and profitable that suggestion is going to be. I will say don't brush it off so fast. Sleep on that suggestion for a few days and if it still feels like it is not useful, let it go.

- ## Be Ready to Fail

  The idea of being wrong shouldn't scare you from trying something new. We fail and we learn. But we never learn anything by avoiding something because of our fear. Weighing the relevancy of a new idea, even if you don't like it determines the rate at which you are going to learn new things and grow.

  Even if you fail at something new that you have tried, at least it will save you from all those nightmarish dreams of "What if?" You know those "What if" thoughts that come and haunt us every now and then. What if I had accepted that job offer? What if I had moved to that city? What if I had married that other person? What if I had digitally transformed my business ten years ago?

We regret more what we have not done than what we have done. So, be ready to fail!

• Be Flexible and Stop Resisting

Flexible minds are the ones which come up with the most ideas. If you're wondering how to become more flexible, I will say start by asking more questions and making less statements.

If you think somebody has said something that you don't agree with, don't say, "This is not possible" or "You're wrong," instead ask a few questions that you think are important in determining the feasibility of that suggestion to clear any doubts.

Let's say your employee suggests you upgrade your supply chain process by using some kind of new technology. If you think it is going to be costly, ask how much that would be and how a small business owner like yourself can obtain that kind of money. In case it is affordable, ask how much downtime will it lead to. Keep asking until all your concerns are answered.

When you ask questions, you make the situation easier. If you're wrong, you would figure out exactly where you went wrong or what you had failed to see that the other person did. If the other person is wrong, your questions would make them realize how realistic that suggestion was.

Let's take this for example. If you're a small business owner, I suggest you start social media marketing for your products. Now, instead of saying that won't work for my business, ask some questions to clear your doubts.

"How is social media marketing even helpful? People don't go there to buy products they are there to socialize."

Pooja - People didn't turn on their TV because they were in the mood to shop but TV ads still became one of the most effective forms of advertising. The fact is that most of us are spending a lot of time on social media channels. We can miss other things, but we will hardly miss scrolling through our Instagram or Facebook feed. Wherever your audience is, you need to be there.

"How much will it cost?"

Pooja - It all depends on how fast you want to grow and what all your business goals are. If you want to sell tens of thousands of products through social media, you will need a bigger budget than if you want to just sell a hundred products. Similarly, if you want to reach people just in Brooklyn, the budget is going to be comparatively smaller than when you want to reach people in the entire US.

"I offer a B2B product. I find it hard to imagine that people will buy a product like that through social media channels." Pooja - Do you know that most of the B2B companies are actively using social media marketing to reach more and more clients? LinkedIn is gaining a lot of popularity for attracting B2B leads.

As you can see, you will learn a lot more when you start asking important questions rather than just making statements.

● Get Ready to Be Challenged

You want to become more open-minded, challenge your ideas without being offended. Don't let your ego ruin your learning experience.

Having your ideas challenged will also lift the clouds of misconception from your mind and you will be able to explore so many new perspectives that you've never seen before.

Encourage others to challenge your ideas. Don't be in a hurry to prove others wrong, only to stick to your views even harder than before. You don't want to satisfy your ego just for the sake of some instant gratification.

Wherever there is a disagreement, there comes in an urge to prove yourself to be smarter, but our actions are not our characters. When I say, "I was wrong," I'm not saying that I am dishonest or less smart than you. I am just acknowledging that what I'd said was not correct and now, I have changed my mind because I have gained more information or a new perspective. It's just showing a desire to grow which is very commendable.

Disagreements are an opportunity to grow and learn something new. It means that you don't care if you're wrong as long as it helps you grow.

The choice is simple: do you want to be right? or do you want to grow?

Get Curious

If you're curious, you will not disregard any other person's suggestion so easily. You will be curious enough to know what that suggestion can do for your business. If it's going to fail, why would it happen? If it's going to succeed, why would it be?

Start the process of becoming more curious by being less judging and more understanding. When somebody's saying something, don't just jump into your defensive mode and start thinking of various ways how you can tell them that they are wrong. On the other hand, think about what will happen if you do what others are suggesting.

Try to see the problem how others are seeing it. It's tough to be wrong especially as the owner of a business, CEO, or the big entrepreneur. It's tough to be wrong when you're leading a team, but I think otherwise. Accepting that you're wrong, shows humility which will set a better example of you as a leader on your team than sticking to something that others can clearly see is wrong.

Changing your mind is not a huge deal. When you change your mind, it just shows that now you have got some new information and because of that new information, now your current understanding of the issue has changed and that's why you now think differently. It doesn't show you're wrong. It just shows you have more information which you didn't have earlier, and your current decision is based on that.

Become a leader that shows humility and not stubbornness.

As it's okay to be wrong.

References

1.https://nypost.com/2016/03/08/20-times-in-history-people-were-really-really-wrong-about-technology/

CHAPTER 2

Failure to Know Your Own Business

"Suspecting and knowing are not the same." — *Rick Riordan, The Lightning Thief*

The Story of Confusion

A long time ago in a galaxy far away, there was a skincare company. Let's call it "ABC." ABC was very excited because they were launching a new product that they thought would bring a revolution in the existing skincare market. They'd spent money in technology, even in marketing and advertising. The area where they didn't spend a dime was market research. They depended solely on the internet articles for their research and even those articles were mainly limited to the first page of the search engines.

But the internet searches alone aren't enough.

Search engines' results aren't always trustworthy. As a matter of fact, they can be easily manipulated.[2] Google claims that it organizes the information in its mission, but it is not doing that, it is also deciding how to present that information to its audience. Let's take for example, Google's autocomplete search feature. The company removes controversial suggestions there but sometimes that controversial information can be the missing piece of a puzzle. In addition to that, a majority of the articles can be just people's opinions (not even experts from that field) presented as facts to others. The sad part is opinions can be incorrect and basing anything on this information can be extremely deadly.

Moreover, most of the algorithms are designed to show you similar articles to what you've just read there rather than presenting you with the complete picture or showing you the other side of the same issue. Algorithms love showing you results that match your ideas, but they may or may not be true. If you think rice is not fattening, you will only find articles in support of that. If you think otherwise, the algorithm will start showing you the other kind of result. In every case, you see only part of the painting.

Research on one kind of skincare product can't be completely applied to all skincare products. Every product has its own set of audience and this audience may not coincide with the entire skincare market. For example, I love lipsticks, but I don't like eye shadows. So, I'm in the market for lipsticks but not in the market of eye shadows. In case you've read research about the lipstick market and then try to target me for your eyeshadow product, you won't be able to convert me as your customer and many others like me. This will lead to wasting your marketing budget.

Internet articles can be used to give direction to your research, but the real research will start after that. You can read The New York Times, The Washington Post, Forbes, Economic Times, or Entrepreneur as much as you want but these still can't replace market research.

Now, you must be wondering how did "ABC" perform if they made so many mistakes?

Within months of launching that business, their failure became inevitable. They'd struggled for a few years, continued forcing their products on the audience, hoping they will start loving it one day. Unluckily, as they'd continued ignoring the audience, the audience continued to ignore their product as well. And very soon, they were wiped off the market.

Inaccurate market research always leads to a business wipe-out.

As you can see, the company made three major mistakes.

First Mistake

The only research ABC did was mainly done for the luxury skincare market as they were under the impression that they are launching a luxury product. But when they didn't see much scope of converting luxury buyers into their regular customers, they'd decided to keep the product unchanged and change the market from luxury to non-luxury. They switched to a totally new audience without understanding their preferences and needs. After all, non-luxury buyers and luxury buyers shop products very differently because they have different needs.

Second Mistake

They did research in one field and applied the results to the other field without realizing that they can't just expand their research results to every industry. Footwear, apparel, accessories, cosmetics - they all belong to the ecommerce category or retail category, but they all are very different industries and require their own research. Even in the area of skincare, lipsticks will need totally different research than eyeshadows. The skincare market in New York City will be different from the skincare market in India.

Third Mistake

After a few months, the results continued to perform unsatisfactory, the company decided to do a little survey to learn how the customers are responding to their product. The results showed that the majority of the customers had found the product wasn't up to their standards and they'd even explained how the product can be made more desirable. Unfortunately, all those issues raised by the customers were ignored on the basis that they don't represent their ideal audience.

One of the problems that we are seeing in this case, in addition to poor market research, is the rigid thinking on management's part. Listening to the audience means that they have to accept that there is something wrong with the product, which is not an easy thing, but it has the potential to save your business from failure. Anything that can grow your business (ethically) is worth considering.

All these mistakes made by the company, when combined together, increased the gap between what the company was offering and what the customers actually wanted. Had they listened to their customers on time, they would have written an entirely different business story.

Why Does Everyone Keep Talking About Market Research?

Market research has always been a very crucial part of any business. This is not something that needs to be done only when you're launching a new product. This is something that needs to be done at every stage of your business.

Market research is not an add-on feature, it's a necessity for business survival and business success.

In other words, market research is the swiss knife for the survival of any business.

The moment you will start considering market research as an ongoing process of your business, you will start uncovering so many hidden insights. From preparing you to handle any kind of unexpected surprises to driving you on the road to business success, you will be surprised to see what all it can do for you.

Even though market research lays the foundation of a business, it's surprising how many people still ignore market research and consider it as an activity that will just waste their money. Such thinking arises when business owners try to weigh the money that they have to pay for market research with its short-term results and not with its long-term benefits. It might not bring you sales in the first few months, but it will help you hold your ground when the going gets tough.

After a few years, when you find that your business is still there when all the others around you have disappeared or are struggling to maintain their existence, remember to thank your market research team.

I have worked with many businesses and 99% of the time I have dealt with businesses who ignored market research as a whole or relied on poor and ineffective market research.

They'd heard a voice in their head that gave them a business idea and they just started working on it. Unfortunately, it doesn't work that way. You might think that your business idea is the best and you will be owning a billion-dollar company very soon, but your audience can still disagree. To emphasize, what your audience has to say about your product matters more than what you have to say about it. Only when your audience's views match yours, you are then able to embark on a journey to business success. But don't get defensive as I am not saying that you should not follow your passion. All I'm saying is, tamed passion works better in the long run.

Understanding Market Research

Before I explain how market research can help your business, it's good to clear any kind of doubt you have related to what exactly market research is.

Market research is the process by which a business gathers and studies information related to the product or service it is providing or the market it is operating in. The process generally starts with collecting unbiased information from various reliable sources using various effective data-gathering techniques. Then that gathered information is studied by market research experts and data scientists who finally convert that rough data into some meaningful information which can be used to gain competitive advantage and to make improved and efficient business decisions.

Enough is Never Enough

Even though most ignored this area of business it's not just important but is sadly never-ending. Market research is not something that you can do one time and then forget about it. It isn't that embarrassing prom.

You need to make it an ongoing part of your business. To put it another way, there is no way out of it.

There is no alternative to market research.

As Rick Rordan said in his quote above, knowing and suspecting are two different things.

You don't want to run your business based on mere suspicions and assumptions.

There is a high possibility that your suspicion is wrong and building a business on false and misleading information can weaken your business and drive you to failure.

For this very reason, forget about the associated costs and time involved in market research and start thinking about how it's going to benefit you in the long-term. When you'll be able to realize that, you will be sitting on a business that can withstand any kind of challenge. You will be sailing smoothly in a boat when everyone around you will either be building their make-shift rafts or drowning in the sea of strenuous business times

The process of research starts with your business idea and lasts as long as your business exists. A successful business owner will know their business as good as they know their favorite celebrity, their partner, and even their dogs.

What Happens When You Ignore Market Research?

1. You Waste Your Time on Ineffective Ideas

Let's say you have come up with a business idea which already exists, all by accident. In a case like that, the market research will make you aware of already existing products and how they are performing in the market. It will tell you what the strengths and weaknesses of those existing businesses are. Once you become informed of that, you can use those points for differentiating your business from others. This way you will not be just another similar business, but you will be a unique player in the same industry.

I have once worked with a company who was launching a mobile app. They had failed to do the initial market research. Upon researching, they learned that there was an already similar product in the market. Surprisingly, the other product was launched by a giant corporation but didn't gain much popularity. It should have made them wonder two things:

-   Why did a product launch by a giant corporation not become popular? Is the product not right or is there something about the product that customers didn't like?
-   Why didn't the big corporation discontinue their product? Does that mean there is still a scope in this line? Are they working on launching the second version which will be better than the first version? What is missing in this product that they are trying to add in the second version?

No market research was done to understand these questions and the senior management decided to go ahead with the project. They'd justified it with the argument that there is always a scope for a second player specializing in the same product just like Uber and Lyft. But what they failed to see is that:

-   Launching a similar product still needs some kind of differentiation. Customers don't just switch from one popular and trusted product to a new and unknown one, even if the two products are the same.
-   If a giant corporation with a huge marketing and advertising budget is not able to gain customers for that product, how are they planning to achieve the different results with their comparatively insignificant budget? In the end, they're both competing for the same customer set. They needed a strategy based on research that can prepare them to compete with the leaders irrespective of their disadvantageous position in terms of their budget.

Coming to the Uber and Lyft story, Lyft was launched very strategically and marketed wonderfully at a time when Uber was busy repairing its brand image because of all the scandals - sexual harassment, loss of executives and more surrounding it.[3]

Lyft provided a substitute product for those who don't want to be a part of an unethical work culture that became associated with Uber in those days. That was the point of differentiation. They were never exactly the same product. While Uber was more a business-like limo car sharing, Lyft was more casual. Though with time, that distinction has become less prominent, but this definitely helped them in the starting stage.

2. You Misunderstand Market and Demand

Demand is one of those factors which decide the fate of your business. It can be the present demand or the future demand.

Your audience is changing every moment and so are their preferences. What they liked yesterday they don't like today. What they like today, they are not going to like to-morrow.

Haven't we all loved Nokia at one point in time?

Always remember that your audience is not made up of bots. They don't follow fixed algorithms and make decisions based on that.

Your audience is made up of humans who are shaped by beliefs and perceptions. Those beliefs and perceptions are never constant. They change as they gain more and more experience of their surroundings. As a result, to make sure that you don't miss the boat to business success, make sure to never stop learning more about your audience.

In the 80s, Colgate launched frozen dinner, but it failed miserably. Can you imagine frozen dinner by Colgate?[4]

It's tough and weird. You know why? Their products have strong brand associations with oral hygiene which makes it so tough for their audience to relate Colgate brand with food.

Had they understood their audience and their perceptions ahead of time, they would have saved themselves from this product failure. They had learned the hard way that changing brand association is not so easy. It's always fun to learn from other people's experiences.

3. You Are Shaken Up by Threats

Market research not only helps you in gaining competitive advantage, but also helps you in being prepared to handle any testing business times. Businesses are made up of various entities. Most of those entities are not constant. Everything is changing, especially the business environment.

Political changes can affect your business. Technical advancements can shake your business off. Presently, we are seeing a wave of environmental changes. Customers are becoming more and more concerned about the environment. They don't want to associate themselves with any product or brand which is not working hard to protect the environment.

Equally important, learning about any kind of changes on time gives you a head start over your competitors which helps you not just in surviving the changes but also emerging as a leader in the end.

4. You Fail to Understand Your Customers

Consider selling a luxury cruise ticket to Henry David Thoreau. Do you think this is something that can be achieved? Heck no!

The reason is very simple. He was never an ideal customer for this kind of business line. While taking into consideration his minimalist, idealist and simplistic lifestyle, he would've never shown an interest in anything luxurious. If you fail to see that and continue targeting him, you will end up just wasting your money without receiving the expected results.

To understand who will be fit for your product, you have to first understand your ideal customers' needs, wants and preferences. To demonstrate, I am a vegan, but I will go to any restaurant but vegan ones. Isn't that interesting? Can you guess what makes me choose other restaurants over vegan restaurants when there is a perfect match in my dietary needs and those restaurants' offerings? It is the inability of most of the vegan restaurants to differentiate between the needs of a vegan who never had meat and a vegan who is not born as one but became one with time. Vegans like me prefer vegetables over fake meat products and this is something which we always find a lack of in vegan restaurants, (feel free to pitch me this idea if you ever see me strolling on the streets of Brooklyn).

This shows the importance of understanding your audience in your business growth. The more you are going to learn about them, the better you will be able to solve their problems and the more interest they are going to take in your product.

5. You Underestimate Your Competition

How many times does it happen when your competitor takes a jump in the game by adapting to something new that you wish you had done first? Have you wondered how your competitor was able to take those leaps? The answer is steroids. I mean market research. I also mean that market research is the safest form of steroids out there.

Proper market research keeps you informed on what your competitors are doing, as well as their strengths and weaknesses. If you know their strengths, you can differentiate on some other unique features of your product. If you know their weaknesses, you can capitalize on it for your gain. In short, remember in the world of business, you keep your friends close but your enemies even closer.

Microsoft launched Zune, something like Apple's iPod in 2006 but their product failed badly. You want to know why? Because they couldn't give customers any reason why they should buy Zune and not iPod.[5] Had they done proper competitive analysis and market differentiation from the very beginning, they would have saved themselves a huge pile of cash.

6. You Exhaust Your Resources

You have limited resources - money, time, employees, raw material and other things. If you manage them well, you can see good results before you run out of them. Market research helps you understand the need of your product in the existing market and the current competition. It also determines how much effort will be required to gain customers and the amount of time needed to become profitable.

If market research shows that the resources required for your idea can only last for four years without any money coming in. Then, it prepares you to get positive ROI before those four years are over. Everything is limited. You will run out of time as well. If you take way too long, your audience will lose interest in your product or somebody else will copy your idea and launch it with some changes.

Not to mention, your employees will get burnt out as well if a project is dragged for too long without any signs of progress. In addition, you have to pay them whether you have started making money or not. This implies that as long as you can afford their pay slips, they will be working on your project otherwise you will just end up exhausting your human resources in addition to your money.

7. You'll Miss Profitable Opportunities

If you invest in market research, you'll learn about valuable business and market opportunities on time which you can use for staying ahead in the game. When it comes to opportunities, timing is very important. If your competitor uses an opportunity for its advantage before you do, you can lose your position as a market leader.

Kodak once failed to adapt to the time of digital cameras and it's paying the price for that even now.[6] The lack of market research at that time has costed them billions and loss of their position in the market. Not forgetting the fact that cameras are still referred to as kodak in rap and R&B songs.

8. You'll Miscalculate the Complexity of Bringing a Cultural Change

This is a major factor responsible for failed businesses. I have seen business owners get so obsessed with their idea that they forget to see whether that idea will be easily accepted by the market or not, whether the idea needs bigger cultural change or just a slight push. A bigger cultural change means you will be taking a bigger risk plus you will need a larger number of resources to achieve that.

You can't just come up with an idea that people should have rattlesnakes as pets, you are working on something that is not done. Consequently, it will need a bigger team, a better strategy, a lot of marketing, highly creative advertising and a longer time frame to implement everything provided the market research which speaks in favor of the idea.

The change from shopping in-stores to shopping online didn't happen overnight. It was a big cultural change which took many years. In the beginning, people were not so comfortable sharing their payment details online like they are now. They found the entire concept risky and untrustworthy. Not being able to feel and touch the product also hampered the success of ecommerce businesses in those days.

Soon, customers started seeing the convenience that online shopping brings, the ease of returns, and the unending varieties they can explore. And with that, the cultural shift started happening. They had started enjoying the comfort of being able to shop whenever they want. Time-starved people were now able to shop in their free time, from the subway, from the restaurant, or from their own homes. They were no longer required to travel to a nearby store only to learn that the store is out of the exact product they had wanted - the size would be missing, the color wouldn't be right. But they would still settle down for one because they don't want to spend any more time driving and looking through their collection again.

So, if you want your customers to start eating spinach flavored ice cream, your idea won't need as much cultural change as it will if you want your customers to start taking a coffee pill in the morning instead of fresh brewed coffee. Obviously, the latter will require more efforts and more marketing.

9. Your Decision-making Becomes Clouded by Your Emotions

The future of your business depends on what kind of decisions you are going to make. The better decisions you make, the better your business is going to perform. The challenge is that the decision-making process is not as simple as it seems.

The process of decision-making can become efficient and effective, if the right information is handy on time. Based on market research, you can develop improved business processes, improve your business performance, increase customer satisfaction and so much more.

After the success of Avatar, many TV companies launched 3D TVs, thinking that people loved Avatar, so they are going to love 3D TVs as well.[7] But this concept failed. The problem is that our assumptions are not always right and there can't be anything more fatal to a business than making decisions based on somebody else's assumptions.

Being successful is not that tough, you just need a little mindset change.

It requires that you understand the importance of those businesses' processes which actually form the foundation of your business and then invest in those. Instead of assuming that there is a need for your product, go test it out. Instead of thinking your customers are going to love your product, go ask them. Instead of thinking that people will easily change their ways of doing a thing and will easily switch to your product, research if they agree to what you feel.

Given these points, I want you to start learning from the mistakes of others right now. You have spent so much time and energy working on your dream business and failure should not be an option now. Incorporate market research as an integral part of your business, and you'll not just become competitive, but also profitable.

Remember market research is like warming up. It will keep you safe from unnecessary injuries.

References

2.https://www.wsj.com/articles/how-google-interferes-with-its-search-algorithms-and-changes-your-results-11573823753
3.https://www.firstpost.com/business/ubers-is-losing-market-share-to-lyft-series-of-scandals-from-sexual-harassment-to-bribery-allegations-does-it-in-4469901.html
4.https://www.thedrum.com/news/2017/08/15/the-failure-awards-defunct-branding-1-colgate-beef-lasagne
5.https://www.businessinsider.com/robbie-bach-explains-why-the-zune-flopped-2012-5
6.https://hbr.org/2016/07/kodaks-downfall-wasnt-about-technology
7.https://www.extremetech.com/electronics/243280-3d-tv-finally-blessedly-mercifully-dead-will-vr-follow-suit

CHAPTER 3

Failure to Plan for Success

"By failing to prepare, you are preparing to fail." — Benjamin Franklin, Founding Father of the United States

The Story of a Failed Blogger

One day I'd received a call from my friend. He was telling me that he had decided to start a food blog where he can share recipes and reviews of various products. He was extremely confident to make a profit in a few months by obtaining some promotional and influential deals. Let me break down his story further so you'll understand all the mistakes that led to this failure:

- Saw other food lovers earning a livelihood through blogs and decided to open his own blog in the same category.

- Blogged for two-three months but then didn't see any revenues being generated. Then lost interest and dropped the idea.

Top bloggers are earning over $100,000 per month!

Who wouldn't want to start a blog after learning that?

A little secret for you. Even I had.

Actually, I had started three different kinds of blogs and failed at every single one of them. My first blog was about books. I would regularly blog about the books I'd read and shared my reviews, opinions, and insights gained from those books along with book recommendations for a few months. But I had failed to attract any audience to my blog. Getting any kind of partnership deals seemed like a distant question! After dragging my book blog for a few more months, I'd decided to let it go.

Then, I thought of starting a new blog about marketing. That one didn't last even for two months. After these two blogs, I had thought of starting a vegan recipe sharing blog. The same story. Everything started with too much enthusiasm. I'd blogged every single day. Uploaded pictures on Instagram more often than that. Then, after a few months I'd realized that even now nobody visits my blog. How would I ever make money from a blog, if nobody visits that blog? I did a little promotion on my social media handles. Nothing much changed even after that. For a day or two, I got 1-10 visitors and then it became a no man's island again. With that, my motivation hit the floor, enthusiasm vanished into thin air and I was back to square one.

What my friend and I forgot to see was that we had tried to enter an already saturated market with an undifferentiated product. Something like that has never made anyone a top blogger. Not planning enough is like preparing for failure even if you are extremely passionate about your idea. Everyone starts a business with passion, but not everyone starts it with enough planning.

That's the difference you will see between a successful entrepreneur and a failed entrepreneur.

A failed entrepreneur has just passion but a successful one knows how to plan to keep that passion alive.

You need a proper plan to figure out the difference between a good idea and a good but already existing idea. If only all of us would focus more on planning, then we won't have so many abandoned blogs and websites (including my three abandoned blogs, two abandoned websites and a dozen of abandoned social media handles)!

You need planning at each and every stage if you want to succeed.

You need to plan how to launch a product, how to secure funds, how to promote, market and advertise, how to manage budgets, how to reach goals, how to gain web traffic, how to turn that traffic into leads and leads into customers, how to keep those customers happy, how to build loyalty and a lot more.

Randomness rarely works for businesses.

The more you plan, the more you will know the likelihood of your idea being successful, the time needed for that and the other resources required. If your plan was just to start a blog and hope somebody will contact you to promote their products, that's like sitting under an oak tree with your mouth open and waiting for the berries to fall in. Which happens once in a million years.

Understanding the Connection Between Business Planning and Business Success

"The general who wins the battle makes many calculations in his temple before the battle is fought. The general who loses makes but few calculations beforehand." -Sun Tzu

You don't go into a war unarmed and without any strategy. (We don't love or support war, so let's try another example). Let's say that you're at a party and your eyes get caught by a person of your dreams. What do you do? How do you approach that dream person standing right there? Do you ask your other common friends to introduce you or do you rehearse what you're going to say first? Whatever you do, everything forms a part of planning and strategy. If you get a date with that person, your planning and strategy has worked. If not, your plan was not that great. Dating is a big battlefield and proper planning becomes important to survive.

If you want to succeed and leave your competitors behind, you need great plans and even greater strategies.

Every step in a business is very important and needs proper planning. This even includes your exit strategy.

Before you decide to launch a project, you need a mission, vision and an action plan that helps you achieve success. Not just that, you also need a plan B and exit plan when things don't go as you planned as you want to reduce your risk as much as you can. In addition, you also need a plan for marketing, sales, business growth, employee motivation, business partnerships, vendor management, client and customer success, brand loyalty, brand image and many others. In short, business is all about planning and then successful implementation of the same.

Small businesses and inexperienced entrepreneurs still continue to overlook the importance of effective business planning. When you come up with an idea, you start with a business plan. You don't just jump into the industry without a parachute. You figure out your goals, financial planning and budget, competitor analysis, marketing, advertising, hiring of employees and so on. Many businesses have failed and continue to fail because they didn't realize the importance of a business plan and how it helps in bringing their businesses closer to their financial goals.

Having a plan B also makes you aware about how realistic and feasible your business ideas are. In the stories above, if my friend would have worked on his business plan and had done a little competitive analysis as a part of that, he would have learned that there was not much scope for his idea as the market is full of similar and better ideas. As a result, he had entered the market with false expectations and was surprised when the success didn't follow in a few months. The same applies to even my failure story.

Planning and Expansion of a Business

Another common reason why many businesses fail is because they start expanding even before they become ready for it. Any kind of business expansion needs a lot of resources. Indeed, it's time consuming. Often times, business owners invest heavily in their business expansion even before their first target market has started generating the expected profits. In cases like this, business owners get their resources stuck in two projects causing both to fail eventually.

I'd once worked with a business owner who had made the same mistake of launching his project in a second country even before the first country started delivering results. The outcome? The same employees were now contributing half of their time in the expansion. Many budgets were cut down so the expansion can be made possible. Time was heavily compromised. After many months of work, it became unsustainable. Employees were overworked and underpaid. Their motivation was going down as the budget was going down. None of them were performing well. Both projects needed additional marketing and advertising budgets, more employees and more time. To tell the truth, for increasing the budget the business owner needed revenue from any one project, but he had none at hand. Finally, both the projects died as the resources dried up.

Overexpansion is counterproductive when you don't have enough resources to sustain that. In the same manner, even rapid business growth. For instance, let's say you have started an ecommerce start-up and your resources allow you to process a maximum of one hundred orders a day. If suddenly, you start receiving a thousand orders a day it wouldn't go too good. It feels amazing to know that there is an increased demand for your product, but customer experience and satisfaction are consequential for long-lasting business growth. An increased number of orders will need more raw materials, more time, and more team members to work on those. You have to do all of this very smoothly without affecting the brand experience of any customer. If your customers become frustrated, then they will switch to somebody else's product and you don't want to give them an excuse to do that.

How to Keep Your Eyes on the Goal at All Times

Let's imagine that I am having a huge party at my place. I send out invitations to you and a few other people to be a part of the coolest party ever thrown. The problem is that I forgot to add my address to the invitation. Sadly, you don't know where I live, and you don't even have a map of my place. What's going to happen next?

You want to become a part of that party but without any destination to arrive at, you find yourself completely lost. Maybe you will take some guesses based on your limited knowledge of where that party can be. Maybe you will turn to Google to know more about it, but you won't find anything relevant. Maybe you will even try to search that place based on your guesses but will never reach the destination. Every action that you will take will just lead to loss of time and energy in figuring out something which shouldn't be so tough in the first place.

Vision and mission metaphorically represent the address that I'd forgot to add in my "invitation." Alternatively, they represent the final destination of your business.[7] If you want your team to reach that destination, you have to make them aware of what your future plans are which are generally defined in your mission and vision statement. In case you want to share more than just the destination, let's say you want to share the map with your team, so they reach the destination quicker, then you have to prepare an action plan as well.

Defining Vision, and Mission for Your Business

The question that will be roaming in your head at the moment will be 'What exactly is vision and mission?' In simpler words, they are the future plans of your business. They show what your business objectives are and what kind of approach you are going to use to achieve them.

Before you embark upon this journey of your business' vision and mission discovery, there are a few questions that you need to answer:
- Why are you in this business?
- How big do you want your business to be one day?
- Who is going to benefit from your product or service?
- What is the core purpose of the existence of your business?

Once you are done figuring out the answers to the questions above, you have to now focus on your company's culture, values and beliefs. Make sure that this reflects in your prepared mission and vision statement.

The easiest way of doing that is by treating your business as a human being. Gone are the days when companies used to be unapproachable to their customers. The internet has helped a lot in bridging the gap between businesses and their customers.

Customers don't want to interact with snobby, cold-hearted businesses who engage in just one-way communication.

Customers want someone just like them, even when it comes to picking a company.

So, it's time to add some values to your business and give it a bigger purpose in life than just making money and increasing sales.

Vision and Mission for Business Growth

Vision and mission contribute to your business' growth in various ways.[8] With a few of those being:
-     Building customer relationships
-     Uniting your team
-     Guiding strategic decision-making process
-     Defining goals and action plans
-     Improving communication with your customers
-     Giving clarity to your business objectives

Common Mistakes Business Owners Make

-     Not Having a Vision and Mission

    Majority of the small business owners don't have any mission and vision statement as they are not able to see the importance of these two and how they shape the future of their businesses.

    Well-defined mission and vision statements are going to show your audience what your business stands for and how it is going to benefit them. When your audience relates to your business' values, it helps in building an instant connection. This leads to long-term, profitable brand-customer relationships.

    Furthermore, your team will be able to see the bigger picture of your business of which they are a part of.

This will make it easier for them to visualize how their work is going to contribute to that vision, giving them a direction as well as a destination. Most importantly, when all your team members have the same vision, they become united by a shared goal. When your team is united and working for the same goals, magic happens.

- ## Having an Unclear Vision, and Mission
Sometimes the problem is not the absence of a mission and vision statement, the problem is how it is written. If your team is going to find it unclear and vague, they will fail to understand it as well as adopt it in their day-to-day work lives.

Here's how to make your vision and mission statement better:

- ### Don't Use Complicated Jargon-filled Words
As preparing a mission and vision statement is still considered an unwanted task, that's why it's still prepared by many in a hurry without much consideration. As a result, many end up putting all the business jargon together and end up calling it their mission and vision.

This statement is not just for your team but is also for your customers and your customers don't have as good industry knowledge as you have. That's why it becomes obligatory to write a mission and vision statement in simpler words.

- ### Don't Make It Generic
A mission and vision statement should be tailored according to your business, its goals, and its needs. As your business is unique, your statement also needs to be. It has to reflect who you

are and how you are different from others.

- Don't Let It Be Vague

  Your team will have a tough time understanding your confusing and obscure missions and vision statement. Eventually, this will make them feel disconnected from your business goals and the purpose of your business. Or they will come up with their own interpretations which might not match yours.

  This kind of disconnection will eventually lead to demotivation.

  Remember, demotivation is highly contagious.

Write your business' aspirational description in a clear and concise manner. Then, communicate it to your team members in a way that helps them grasp it in a way that makes them feel connected with it. Soon, you will find your team using your mission and vision statement for guidance whenever they are confused or lost.

A good vision will not just give your employees much-needed direction but also much-valued inspiration to do their work efficiently.

Build a Boat When There is No Flood

As it might not be easy to build a boat when you are drowning. You'll want to work on your boat when the skies are clear, and the sun is shining. And when there is a flood, you will be ready with your boat to set sail to new land and explore new opportunities. In case your boat isn't ready, you will either drown or will try to build a make-shift boat which might be harder than you can imagine.

Why you should work on your boat (or your business action plan) now.

- It makes it easy to run your business.
- It keeps your goal in line all the time.
- Your decision making isn't influenced by your emotions because suddenly the situation is critical.
- It saves you time.
- It makes your business planning more effective.
- It helps in aligning your business goals with your customer values.
- It refines your business strategies - marketing, growth, sales, customer satisfaction, client success and more.
- It assures that you expand your business only when the time is right.

The Art of Planning for Failure

It's so surprising that we prepare our businesses for the best times, but we forget to prepare them for the worst times. A business life is just like a human life. There are happy times and then there's bad times. We don't go down when tough times strike us, but we fight back and survive. Interestingly, we even prepare ourselves for tough times by securing health, car, house and life insurances. If we could only do the same thing for our businesses, they'd live much longer and useful lives.

We've been trained to focus solely on the booming times of a business and overlook anything that doesn't present the same rosy picture.

"Tornadoes never hit this part of the city."

"All our data is backed up so efficiently, we can never have a data breach."

"Pandemic? Are you kidding me? We're so medically advanced that a pandemic like or worse than 1926 is unimaginable."

We need to be hopeful. This is a part of the surviving spirit, but we also need to be realistic and accept that unexpected things happen more often than we believe. We are not accepting our defeat by doing that; we are just accepting this so we can work on our survival plan.

Not having a contingency plan or never performing risk analysis and mitigation activities is like not having an insurance plan for yourself. If any tragedy strikes, you will not be able to handle it well.

Do You Even Need a Plan B?

COVID 19 Business Lesson

COVID-19 has affected our businesses in in numerous ways that we've never even imagined.[9] From interrupting important business travel to breaking down the critical life-supporting supply chains, it has made it tougher for any business to survive.

If there is anything important that a business owner could learn from this pandemic is to always be prepared for the unexpected. As of Aug 31, 163,735 businesses have been marked as permanently closed down on Yelp.[10]

163,735! This is not a small number which can be overlooked. This is also not a number that you can just ignore and convince yourself that nothing much could have been done. This is a number that tells you that you have to learn to fight and most importantly, learn to survive and thrive better than ever before.

Many more businesses will close down in the next few months. About 75% businesses fail within three years after a major disaster.[11]

This implies that the number of businesses closing down at the moment, doesn't include all and this number is going to go way up high. The result of this pandemic on businesses who didn't have any plan will be seen in many years to come.

These unwanted and unexpected situations are so uncommon that it doesn't seem useful to spend our time and energy in figuring out what to do if something unfortunate happens. But your contingency plan is as important as your business plan. As many of these businesses could have fought better, many could have survived as well, had only they have known the importance of having a contingency plan.

What is a Contingency Plan/ Plan B?

A contingency plan is an action plan or a risk mitigation plan for a business when uncertainties strike. These uncertainties can be natural disasters or manmade disasters. It can be a flood, tornado, fire, pandemic, political change, industrial regulation, active shooters, data breaches, network outages, injury, death, financial loss, reputation loss or something else.

A contingency plan is a plan that helps you continue your business when times are not as good as you had expected. It is your plan to prepare yourself for the absolute worst that can happen. When things go wrong, this plan will guide you toward survival.

As a matter of fact, most of these disasters are out of your control but that shouldn't stop you from creating your contingency plan. When you will find yourself all confused and unable to make a decision, this plan is going to help you respond to unfavorable situations and to make sure that your business continues running smoothly.

The Need for a Plan B or Exit Plan

You can't cover all the disasters in your contingency plan, so you should focus on only those ones that are more common for your business and your business location. If your business is not in a flood-prone area, you don't have to include it in your plan. Similarly, if you are selling a product whose final cost in a competitive market is dependent on the cost of raw materials, then you should include inflation in your plan.

A contingency plan is also known as your plan B and it's always good to have an alternate plan of action when things don't go as planned. Imagine when your boat starts shaking up because of the rough weather and big waves but instead of steering your boat through this, you are taking a break and working on your strategy of action. Doesn't seem good, right? Every second is crucial here.

The same thing applies for your business in difficult times. Are you going to steer your business out of it or are you going to leave your business in it while you work on a plan? Every second in such times is either moving you toward failure or survival. Better and faster decisions, unaffected by the emotional turmoil that you and your business is going through, can decide your fate.

Moreover, the environment where we operate our businesses is continuously evolving. Sometimes this environment takes a big plunge before touching unachievable heights of societal betterment. If we are able to survive that plunge, we will soon find ourselves at those heights but if we are not prepared for that plunge, we will be wiped off. In a way, it's just the survival of the fittest. A contingency plan is going to prepare you not just to fight disastrous situations but also emerge out of it stronger and better rather than frail and weak.

What's Your Plan B?

A contingency plan is not as tough as it seems. It's a four-step process.
- Identify a risk or threat.
- If you can avoid it, go for it.
- If you can't avoid it, is there a way you can mitigate it? If yes, create your action plan for that and implement it whenever such scenarios arise.
- In case you can't avoid that risk or even mitigate it, then the smart decision is to accept it.

Disasters Don't Believe in Excuses or Second Chances

Markets crash!
Disasters happen!
A pandemic can come anytime!

We have to get rid of this stigma attached with a contingency plan. When you prepare for the worst it doesn't mean that you don't have enough confidence in your business idea, it just means that you're smart enough to know that accepting the unexpected is the first most important step of fighting it.

Real business leaders stay calm when calamity happens because they have prepared for situations like these. They have a plan B. They have a backup plan. When others are thinking about what to do next, they are implementing their plan and moving ahead of others.

In the end, your business is built on proper planning. Starting with your business plan to your contingency plan, it all makes your business stronger. Many businesses fail because the owner loses motivation and enthusiasm. That generally happens because the expectations are not kept in check. Unrealistic expectations arise when no proper planning was done to show the correct picture.

Believing that your blog idea will make you a millionaire, when it can't even bring you hundreds of dollars isn't a solution. The solution lies in proper planning. A good plan can show you that your idea can bring you hundreds currently but if you tweak this idea a little and target this particular set of customers with this particular form of marketing strategy, in a few years you can bring thousands and may be in another couple of years tens of thousands. This seems more realistic.

A business plan shows you the right path. It tells you which road is going to take you where you want to go. Can anything be more important than working on your own business?

References
8.   https://www.bizadmark.com/writing-business-mission-statement/
9. https://www.pnas.org/content/117/30/17656
10.https://www.cnbc.com/2020/09/16/yelp-data-shows-60percent-of-business-closures-due-to-the-coronavirus-pandemic-are-now-permanent.html
11.   https://visual.ly/community/Infographics/business/business-disaster-preparation

CHAPTER 4

Failure to Create a Good Enough Product to Succeed

"I set out to find bad men, but I couldn't find any. When I finally peeked inside myself, there was no one worse than I am." - Kabir

The Story of Cakes

Who doesn't know a person who either owns a bakery, owned a bakery or plans to own a bakery? I do know at least ten such people.

The interesting thing is that instead of a high business closure rate, people still continue to invest in the bakery business. For the simple reason that it feels good, but it still may not be a good enough product to succeed.

There is nothing wrong with the baking industry. It's not more competitive than any other industries. And in no way am I implying that the world has enough bakers. Neither does the world have sufficient cakes.

I am just saying the industry is right but most of the time the idea or product is not.

One time my friend who was a very passionate baker, decided to start her own bakery. Yes, it was a friend, not me. (Phew!)

She took out a small loan and set up her bakery in Brooklyn. After a year, she discontinued the business. What happened was in the very beginning, she was very much enamored by the idea of doing something that she loves, which is actually a very good thing. You should always do what you love. Although enamored by her passion for baking, she forgot that this world doesn't need just another baker.

The world needs a differentiated baker!

"Can you bake a normal cake?"
People in Brooklyn: Not interested.
Can you bake a cake with Bluetooth?
People in Brooklyn: Can I use my credit card?
(Yes, I know! The second idea is not very realistic, but you get my point and that's what matters.)

Let's say you are planning to open a bakery in my neighborhood meanwhile, there are already many bakeries here. If you open another one, your product wouldn't attract people like me. But if you open the only gluten-free bakery of the town, vegan bakery of the town, or sugar-free bakery, it might work.

People can never get enough of something new and different.

They don't want another option for the same thing. This is no way to compete in a market! Most of the bakers forget that businesses don't thrive on passion. They thrive on differentiation and being unique.

Sprinkle a little bit of passion on a good idea, and then spread some crunchy business plan, and you have got a gold mine.

Make sure to have a strong base before you do that, otherwise it will get soggy under all the extra weight and nobody likes that kind of peanut butter jelly sandwich. (Looks like my train of thoughts derailed at the food stop!)

Always Start with a Clear Vision

You won't develop a successful product, if you don't start with a clear vision.

This vision is going to help you develop a product which people are going to love. For example:

I want to start a bakery. (Not a clear vision.)
I want to start a bakery in Louisville. (Still, not a clear vision.)
I want to start a vegan bakery in Louisville. (The vision is getting clearer.)
I want to start a vegan, sugar-free bakery in Highlands in Louisville specializing in cakes, muffins and breads. (Even better.)
I want to start a vegan, sugar-free bakery in Highlands in Louisville specializing in cakes, muffins and breads because there is only one more similar bakery in the city, but it is not at a convenient location for people residing in Highlands and other neighboring areas. (Neat idea.)

The point to remember - location matters more than you think when it comes to any kind of food business.

A Product Bound to Fail

What if everything is perfect in your business except what you are offering to your audience?
Tough to imagine. Isn't it?

Somehow thinking anything bad about our idea or product is just not well-ingrained in our DNA. We keep sticking to our idea even if it's rejected by most people. We keep making excuses to justify why the product isn't liked this time but will be liked very soon. But that never happens.

Under these circumstances, what happens is that you end up finishing up almost all of your energy, enthusiasm and resources. Then, you're left with no other option but to drop the project. But deep down in your heart, you still don't believe that there was anything wrong with your idea. You still think that the marketing perhaps was not done right, or the advertising budget needs to be bigger, maybe you should have partnered with that Brooklyn based digital marketing agency and not the LA one. Perhaps the product should have been launched a few years ago or a few years after or something else.

In short, something was wrong, without a doubt, but according to you, it was just not your product.

Sometimes the right business decision is to let it go - to let go of an underperforming employee, to let go of an unprofitable branch, to let go of a weak advertising campaign, and to let go of an idea which fails to create the hype you wanted it to be.

Are You Joining or Leading the Crowd?

A wrong product will make you a part of the crowd, but the right product will set you apart.

If you want to lead a crowd, you don't copy. You work on a product which is not there in the market, but the customers desperately need that one. Such products have enormous value to offer to their customers. This creates a great demand which leads to success.

If you're leading the crowd, the profits you can make are un-

limited.

But if you're just following the crowd, then there is a limit to what you can earn in addition to higher chances of your failure.

Does Your Product Involve Cultural Change?

This is something that many entrepreneurs don't think about while working on their ideas. The reality is that this is the only thing which is going to decide how many resources you are going to need.

Let's say you're launching a product which your audience has never used. Let's say you've started an ecommerce website when the internet boom just started. At this time, your audience would have needed more education to overcome the resistance to change. This means you might have been required to market and advertise more.

Such changes won't happen overnight. Big cultural changes will take a lot of time. Sometimes, even more than a year. Sometimes even many years. So, prepare yourself for this if your product falls in this category.

If your product doesn't need much societal change, you can do with lesser resources. This doesn't mean that the second one is a much better option than the first one.

In fact, if your product is bringing a bigger cultural change, it will take time but when that period of resistance is over, you will be able to reach the heights you've never even thought existed like Amazon did.

Why Does Your Product Suck?

This is not something you want to read but it's better to prepare yourself than to regret it later. Reasons why a product doesn't perform good are:

- ## There's No Demand and Value for What You're Selling

  Many times, we continue believing that there is a need for our product just because we find it so amazing. But what we think about our product is not going to help much because we are not our target audience. Think about value, user-friendliness and other features it has to offer to others.

  We have to start listening to what our ideal customers have to say about our product with an open mind. Instead of getting defensive when an unattractive side of our product is brought to light, we have to start thinking of ways to make it better, so the audience loves it even more. In the end, all we have to do is to be in the shoes of our audience and our product will hardly fail.

  The most important purpose of any product is to satisfy a customer's need and not the entrepreneur's need.
  When you start seeing your product as your customer's product and not as your product, you will start seeing all the missing gaps.

  Don't just rely on one form of research for analyzing the needs of your customers. Sometimes one source of information can show us a false picture. Let's take focus groups for an example. They are good but only if they accurately represent your audience. For example, if your product is for women between the ages of 18-50, living anywhere in the US and your focus group is made up of ten women from New York between 30-49, then the results won't be very accurate.

- ## The Product is Either Too Advanced or Too

Outdated

Many times, the idea we come up with is not fit for the current times but if launched at the right time can do wonders. On one hand, our idea can be too ahead in a time, when the audience is not ready for such a big jump. They might have some said and unsaid doubts about that product which will only be solved with the passing of time.

Let's time travel and think of the time when the internet and social media were still new.

During those days, people were worried about sharing their personal pictures with strangers on the internet. They liked keeping their profiles private because of the various risks involved in using the internet.

Imagine if Instagram would have been launched at a time like that, when people were juggling so many safety, security and privacy issues of using the internet and social media. What would have been the response? Now, come back to the present and go on your Instagram. Do you see how comfortable, without an iota of fear, we share our pictures and videos with everyone? The digital world has become safer and with that, came into existence many great ideas.

Sometimes, on the other hand, the idea can be way too outdated. In such cases the audience has either already moved on to a newer and better version of that product, and now there is no point of launching your idea. Or the customers have skipped that intermediate stage where your product is and have leaped to a product stage after that. Even launching your product in this case won't produce any favorable results. We can't go back to big, messy and giant computers, poor internet connection, or black & white TVs.

Either way, the product is not right, and we need to make it more appropriate for the time.

- You're Resisting the Change

Once I was working with a client who was launching a product to beat the technology. Even though the thoughts behind the product were good unfortunately, the idea wasn't.

We fail to understand many times that change is inevitable. The best way to deal with any kind of change is to embrace it. Similarly, when it comes to technology, we have already adapted to it. We can't go back to those times when we used an encyclopedia instead of Google to look something up, sent slow letters and not fast emails to our friends, and used notebooks and not Microsoft Word or Google Docs for our documents. Those were the days when we used to physically store tons of data in various files not backed up on iCloud, and spent countless hours visiting physical stores rather than browsing products on click-away ecommerce stores.

We can't go back because we have moved on.
It's just like dating. Your ex has moved on and so should you. (I mean it.)

Fighting a change and clinging to the same old ways of doing things have never proved to be productive for anyone - you or your customers.

It's bad for your business to refuse change when the technology is changing, but it's worse for your business to fight the technology. If you try to, you will be standing there alone, when your customers will keep moving farther and farther from you.

- Your Product isn't Made for the Real Custom-

ers

Are you building a product for yourself or for your audience? Are you creating something for real humans or nonexistent, imaginary ones? Are you building a product for humans or for bots?

One of the most common reasons for a product failure is poor audience research. **Thinking about what your customers like and what they exactly like are two different things.**
Market research is way more than just saying that my mom liked it.

I can like big cities and you might like suburbs. If you don't ask me what my needs and preferences are, you will never know and will assume that I do too, as everyone loves suburbs.

Another mistake that we can make is seeking answers from people who confirm our already confused views because they have similar views themselves. As a result, this ends up solidifying all our assumptions.

Suddenly a bad idea becomes a perfect idea just because everyone you've talked to has said so. Your family members, relatives, friends and your employees won't openly disagree with your idea either.

But this is not very productive for a business. Your audience is very different from you unless and until you are targeting innovators and entrepreneurs just like yourself, then there can be some similarities otherwise not.

- Pricing Affects Your Product Success

I have met so many people who've underestimated the importance of right pricing which ultimately costed them their business. All the pricing numbers were imagined by my fellow business owners, without any strategy.

Alas! Such products don't survive for too long. You can't just think what you want from your product and start charging the same. Here's why a product without proper pricing strategy fails:

- Charging Too Little

  When we decide the price of our product, we often fail to take into consideration the various kinds of expenses. Consequently, it ends up showing you an inaccurate picture of your profits. Only when you continue making no profits or negative profits, you'll realize that you forgot to consider a few expenses in your profit calculation.

  Let's take the example of the bakery again. When you're calculating the cost of your muffins and how much profit you can make, you have to remember to not just add the cost of ingredients but also include marketing, employee salary, rent, amenities like utility bills, and various other things to figure out the right break even number.

  Other times, when we start a business, we price our services so low even though we have enough experience and expertise to charge a premium. What happens in cases like these is you will get burnt out, you will lose interest because you will find yourself doing too much and not being paid enough for your time.

  You have to remember that even if your business is new, your experience and expertise are not. You have spent many years mastering those skills and charging a price in reflection to those skills is not something you have to think twice about.

- Charging Too Much

Unfortunately, this case is more common than the first one. But people are very smart, they are not willing to pay any unfair price.

Once I was talking to a business owner who had just started an app and the app had no users. Irrespective of that, she tried to charge a high fee to other businesses for advertising there. As can be expected, no business agreed, and it led to the downfall of her business.

The analysis of this entire case is very simple. If you don't have any audience, why would anyone pay you to show their ads on your app? But overpowered by the greatness of her business idea, she couldn't see that.

In another case, a business owner tried to charge for the online services which are generally available for free on other websites. The question here is why would a consumer pay you if they can avail the same services for free on other websites? Either that business owner is supposed to provide something extra or bring the prices down to compete with others. Unluckily, he neither wondered any of these simple questions nor made any amendments. End result - the business ceased to exist.

- ## The Product Needs Higher Resources Than You Can Afford

When you start a product, you need more than money. The four important resources that greatly affects your business idea are:

- ### Funds

Funds, no doubt, play an important role in deciding how long you will last in the market without making any profits. If your product is something complex and will take at least a year in production and a year in raising the brand awareness about it, then you have to make sure that you have funds for at least two years before you jump into the market.

If your products can't last more than a year with the funds you have, then you have to figure out how you are going to make your business profitable in a year's time. If there is no way to earn profits in that time, then you have to let that idea go or wait till you have enough money to start that business. In addition, you have to think about how you are going to procure raw materials at cheaper costs and maintain a profitable supply chain.

- Time

Many of us always forget time as an important resource. It feels like we have unlimited time, but we don't. Every product comes with a time limit. If you delay your product launch, somebody else could launch a similar product in that time, making your product outdated and taking a big chunk of your market share.

If you launch your product way too early before your audience is ready for it, they would end up discarding your product as something unwanted.

I tell my clients, when they approach me for their business growth needs, that they have to decide which one they want to sacrifice to see the growth of their business: money or time?

A business can be grown with the help of right marketing and advertising on a smaller budget, but it will take more time than expected to produce the results as compared to a business with a bigger budget. I generally suggest picking the first option as you can always earn more money, but you can never have more time.

- Human Power

  Your employees play an important role in writing the chapter of success of your product. Before you start working on your idea, you need to know who you need to hire and how you are going to pay them.

- Copied Product Idea or No Differentiation

The only reason your product is not differentiated or is not unique is because you have a copied idea.

The world doesn't need more of the same things.

They need faster, better, cheaper, smoother, easier or something which is a different version of the thing that already exists, in case the idea is not completely new.

Don't make the mistake of duplicating someone else's idea. You need to stand out in the crowd and be unique. This is the only way that can lead you to success. (If you still want to copy someone's idea, upgrade it to the current time and increase its possibility of success.

For example, we don't need another similar car, but we would love to have electric cars which don't require long hours of charging. Maybe there can be some kind of charging stations and we can go there with our dead batteries and replace those with fully charged ones, saving us all the time that is generally spent in charging a car.

- You Stopped Innovating

When you find a good, unique and profitable idea, this doesn't imply that it is going to be unique forever. Many other people are going to capitalize on your success and will launch similar products with better features and services.

Even many big corporations! This ultimately will make your product outdated, more expensive, or not as easy to use as what others are providing.

The solution to not get stuck in a situation like this is to never stop innovating your product. As soon as you hit a good idea, make profits through it, and then, think about what the next version should look like.

- Better and Cheaper Alternatives and Substitutes are Available

We don't have to just analyze our direct competitors, but we also have to analyze our indirect competitors in the form of alternatives and substitutes. You can decide to open a vegan bakery but if cheaper and better vegan baked products are available at grocery stores, then a majority of your audience will just buy those products from the grocery stores rather than your bakery.

- Your Idea is Unprofitable

Sometimes even after having a great idea, you will find difficulties in making money through it. This is mainly because your idea is unprofitable. I'd once worked with a documentary maker. Their idea was amazing. People loved the documentary as well. The only problem was most of the online channels didn't allow monetization of that documentary because of the sensitive topic. The documentary was successful, but it failed to earn them any money.

- Complex Products That People Can't Relate To

Many ideas are just way too complicated that your audience

is not able to relate to that concept. They end up rejecting such ideas. You need a product which can make their lives easier; a product that they need and can relate to as well.

There came many such complex products in the market, but the audience never adjusted to accept that kind of complexity in their lives.

-

What Can You Do to Build a Better Product?

This is a simple four step process that you can easily adapt into how you go about your business.

1. Start with Market Research

Never underestimate the importance of good market research. The results of it aren't instantly visible but this is something that keeps you right on track as well as in the game for longer.

From understanding your audience to knowing your competitors, make sure to make all kinds of research a part of your business.

In the Bible of successful businesses, market research is the holy grail.

Another important thing to remember here is that market research is an ongoing process. Don't just do the research before the product launch but continue doing it even after that. First, you want market research because it tells you whether your audience is accepting to your product or not. Second, you want market research because it will help you in updating your product whenever any change in the need arises. Last, you need market research so you can make your customers happier and solve their problems on time.

2. Learn to Lead the Change

Don't be scared of the changing times. Things are never constant, even if they appear so. In fact, the business environment is made up of so many continuously changing factors that banking your business success and growth on a product which never changes can prove to be detrimental.

I know there are so many emotions attached with your product. Even more, you find it very safe to sell the product that was once accepted in the market. But being safe can prove to be very dangerous. Think about Kodak for a moment.

That's why, you should always keep your focus on leading the change.

3. Don't Be Scared to Take the Risk

Be prepared to take the risks. Even when you see others playing safe, you shouldn't.

Risks and opportunities are different sides of the same coin.

When others are seeing something as a risk, you should see it as an opportunity and capitalize on it.

Once Henry Ford said, "If I had asked people what they wanted, they would have said faster horses." He was not advising that you should stop listening to your customers, but he was saying that many times the needs can be hidden and if you are willing to take risks, you can change the game.

The point is even though he'd moved his customers from horses to cars, he still satisfied their needs for faster transportation. This need was well taken care of by a faster and better option than horses and that's why the audience accepted the risk that he took.

4. Let it Go

If even after doing everything, the product is still not performing good, then the only good thing to do is to let it go. You can save yourself a lot of resources which you can later use for your other entrepreneurship ventures.

Always remember that a product performs good when it has some potential in it. Sometimes even though the product is not right, we still continue believing that all we need our product to be accepted is to reach more people. But that's not the solution, that's just avoiding the problem.

CHAPTER 5

Failure to See the Full Picture of a Business

"I am but a speck of dust in this vast universe." - M. Mondesir

The Story of a Pixel

With the rise of digital cameras and the ease of website creation came the flooding of photographers. Every other person who owned a digital camera wanted to enter the field of professional photography. A lot of those photographers were actually amazing. The problem was that a majority of them mistook their tool or their photography skill for a business.

In simpler words, I can be a great cook, but this doesn't always translate to that I can run a successful restaurant. Otherwise, the world will be overcrowded with 100 times more restaurants. Now, you are going to say that it's not feasible because restaurants require a large investment.

Let's imagine that opening a restaurant has become super easy in the current times, banks are providing loans at a very low interest rate. Now, many of you will still not open a restaurant because you know that running a restaurant and cooking for your family are not the same thing. Somehow, we forget this logic when it comes to industries with extremely low investments like photography. Knowing how to take good pictures and running a successful photography business are very different.

When the entry to a business is easy like it is in the lines of photography, digital marketing, and many others, it confuses many people as an opportunity to try their luck as well. But business is not luck, it's about impeccable strategy and not making the seventeen mistakes talked in this book.

The reason why many people think about opening a photography business and not opening a restaurant is that opening a restaurant involves huge initial investment which keeps their expectations in check.

The field of photography seems easy to enter. When the digital camera wave came, everyone built a website and got a camera. But in a few years, most of them were wiped off the face of the market.

This mainly happened because they thought that the field requires only a camera and a website.

If only they had stepped back and took a look at the bigger picture of how a business is run. It's built on various interconnected processes and all those processes need to perform good if you want to succeed. As much as you need a website, you will also need marketing, advertising, promotion, client servicing and a lot more. You will also need strong budgeting in place, so you don't end up spending more than you make. You need a strong team who can work with you on your goal with the same amount of zeal and passion. No business is just a one man's job. You need sales, you need operations, you need partnerships, you need even customer and brand loyalty.

If you step further back, you will see that now you have various other things that are going to affect your business like the competition in the industry. You will realize that you have joined the crowd of various other people with a website and a camera.

If you want to survive, you need to be different. You have to stand out of the crowd.

Remember, a business is not just your product. It's made up of many layers and all those other layers are also equally as important.

What You Need to Know When Starting a Business

Your idea (which in many cases coincide with your website) is just a speck in the universe of successful businesses. With every step farther away from your idea, you will find something new which will be affecting your business directly or indirectly. The moment you perfect all these things, you will find yourself at a place where this picture will make sense, where your business will avoid failure.

Most of the time, you'll concentrate just on your website but when you take your focus off of it, you'll realize that there's more to a business than that.

You need to work on so many internal factors that affect your business. These will include:

- Human resources so you can hire and train the best employees. You have to train, develop, motivate and build a community of them. They need to become a part of your project even emotionally. They need to see what you see in your project.

- Finance so that you have a realistic budget. So, payrolls can be managed, financial hurdles can be avoided, for a constant smooth cash flow.

- Marketing so people become aware of your products and

consider buying it. This is no doubt the most important step because this is what helps you in building your brand. In addition, you have to manage and retain your brand image.

- Closing sales is a different process altogether. It is as important as marketing. Marketing can bring you the leads but the last step of turning those leads into customers decide the fate of all your efforts. This is known as closing sales.

- Dealing with customers and clients involves completely different sets of businesses processes. You will need to not just aim for customer satisfaction but also for customer delight. You have to work on your customer relationship management.

- Another area is vendor management and partnership management. Even though it seems easy, it's not. Maintaining proper relationships with vendors is very crucial in bringing down the cost of your products and sourcing the perfect raw materials.

- Operations play a major role in customer satisfaction. It involves all those processes that are responsible for making a product. From sourcing of raw materials to production of the actual product, from inventory management to quality management, operations will make sure that the quality product is available to every customer at the right cost, right place and at the right time.

- Competition is ignored so many times that business failure becomes inevitable. Entering a highly crowded market without a unique and new idea is a repeated mistake made by many. When that happens, most of the people find themselves completely exhausted in this process of building their identity and getting noticed in the crowd of many others.

These are the internal factors. However, the businesses are in fact affected by the external environment, too. The external environment of your business is made by all those factors that can affect it outside of the business. These factors are generally not in your control.

- Political environment: Political changes decide various things related to imports and exports, data, privacy, foreign investment and many other things. Sometimes when we start something, we forget to check how the current environment or the future version of it is going to affect our businesses. A sound understanding of that can save you from any kinds of surprises.

- Legal environment: Many times, there are various legal requirements that you have to fulfill before and even after entering the market. Many of us forget to take this into consideration in our business planning.

- Economic environment: How is the economy performing at the moment? Can you get funds at a lower interest rate? Inflation rate? Exchange rate? These are some of the questions that you need to answer. In these digital times when every business is becoming more and more globalized, keeping an eye on the economic environment - not just of your own country but also, of any other country which forms a part of your target market is very essential.

- Social and cultural environment: Our culture shapes our preferences. Not everything can be sold to everyone. Every one of us is similar yet so different. People in India prefer entirely different things from people in the USA or China. Next time you visit a new country, remember to check out their McDonalds (provided it has its restaurant there) and you will see how different everyone's culture is and how these cultures make us adapt our product accordingly.

If you're ambitious, you can bring a cultural change

through your product instead of adapting, in case it leads to a better society and healthier mother earth. But the entire process generally involves a very handsome budget and availability of good amount of time.

- Technological environment: Every day something new is being developed. Everyday all the tech corporations are working on adding new features to their products. Everyday various entrepreneurs are working on their products to change the world. In an ever-changing society like this, technology becomes an important deciding factor for the success of your business.

- Demographic environment: You need to understand your demographics before you choose a location for your business. Not just to decide the labor costs for you but also the kind of products that are in demand. If the labor market is higher in cost, then your production cost will increase as well. If the demographic of your target market is extremely environmentally conscious, then they are going to feel dissatisfied if your packaging is not biodegradable. Learn more about your demographic, so you can introduce a product that aligns their exact needs and philosophy.

A successful business is not built just on your expertise, it needs mastering of all the business pieces and maintaining the interconnection among them in a profitable and fruitful way.

You Need More Than Just Your Product

- ### You need more than a website
  A business will require you to wear many hats. You have to be a leader with a mission, vision and direction. As a leader, you're going to handle the motivation of your team, crisis management, team building, and employee satisfaction. Your leadership skills

will go far beyond your team. You need to work for the betterment of your stakeholders, government and the society.

If you want to be in the business for a long time, you need to work on your skills for client success, relationship building, sales, and customer support. Functional expertise cannot be ignored. It's as important as your leadership skills.

- ## Not seeking professional experience and trying to do it all

It's tempting to try to do everything in hopes to save a lot of money. But this way of working always backfires. It's better to be a master of one than a student of all. It's feasible but you may have to spend many years mastering all those fields you're trying to work on at the same time before you see the right results.

In the words of Malcolm Gladwell, 10,000 hours of practice in any field is the secret number which makes you an expert.[12]

- ## Not Hiring for Administrative Tasks

You have to save your time for more strategic and creative tasks. Anyone can do the administrative tasks, but not everyone can think like you.

Save your energy for the tasks which nobody else can do easily but you.

Limited Knowledge of Business and its Goals

Let me ask you a simple question, why are you starting a business?

    A. To sell products/services
    B. To increase revenue
    C. To increase profit

Majority of the people will say one of the three and this is where everything goes wrong. Before you can decide your business goals, you have to understand what a business is exactly.

Understanding a Business

A business is a value creation and distribution process. What I mean by that is you are not selling a product, but you are selling value to your customers. Before you can sell value to your customers, you have to first create it. Once you're done, you have to distribute it, so your targeted audience becomes aware of it.

The mantra here is the more value you are going to create, the more profitable customer relationships you are going to build thus the more successful your business is going to be.

Understanding Your Role as a Business Owner

As a business owner, your job is to implement the entire process of value creation and generation as effectively and efficiently as you can. Before you start working on your plan on how to create and generate value for your customers through your product, there is something else you need to think about.

Who do you think is responsible for creating the value? Who are you going to assign this task to? Your product team, your marketing team? Or both? Or some other team?

The answer to the question is everyone who is directly or indirectly associated with your business. Value is not always visible. Sometimes, it's invisible and intangible. All the departments in your company work together to generate value. Your product team will work to create a superior product, your HR team will make sure that you are getting the best employees who add more value to your product. Not just the HR department, all the other departments in your company including the finance department, IT department, sales department and any other, are all contributing to that value. Indeed, all these increments when combined together becomes huge.

Not just your internal team, but even your external team is responsible for contributing to this process. Your external team includes your distribution, marketing, advertising, and web partners who are working with you; they all are equally responsible in this process.

What Can Poor Business Understanding Lead To?

Problem 1) I've got an idea

"Unfortunately, it's the same as most others!"

Majority of the time, people are working on an idea that is not unique.

You can't ignore the importance of being unique, remarkable and differentiated in a highly crowded market.

When the customers, just like the business owner, fail to see why they should buy this and not that, a business will collapse.

You must have already seen so many ecommerce websites who sell the same kind of product without any differentiation. If not, just google how many ecommerce websites are out there. I will tell you - there are almost twenty-four-million ecommerce websites in 2020.[13] Now think about how many of those ecommerce websites you're using. Why are the rest not doing as good as others?

To keep it short, the majority of the ecommerce websites are not giving enough reasons to the customers as to why they should pick them over others.

Problem 2) All I need is a website

"Websites and businesses are not interchangeable terms."

There are still so many people out there whose idea of starting a business is merely limited to creating a website. The website gets ready, even before the idea is refined. Too much time and energy has already been spent on just fixing the website, as if the website is enough to convert a lead to a customer.

A business is actually made up of so many important segments and a website is just one of them. If you have mastered your website but all the other areas of your business remain weak, then your product won't perform well in the market.

Sometimes, the opposite of this happens, when business owners pay all their attention in designing and decorating their brick & mortar stores and leave their websites looking like a piece of junk.

Problem 3) My business goal is to make money

"Mutual benefits go farther!'

This is the biggest problem prevalent among the current business owners - the inability to see why they are actually running a business. They fail to realize that they are in the business to satisfy their customers' needs with the help of their products to make their lives easier and better.

If you have any other reason for being in the business other than the above-mentioned, I'm afraid to say you're going to be very disappointed.

Keep your focus on increasing customer satisfaction and building customer relationships, everything else will take care of itself.

Problem 5) This part of business is more important than others

"Weakest link defines the chain."

Business is more than selling.
It's about many units working together to achieve the common shared goal. A business is made up of various branches - finance, HR, IT, marketing, sales, and many others. Sales branch is responsible for directly interacting with the prospects and converting them into the customers. This creates misconceptions among many that the sales department is more important than other departments, but this is not the case.

In reality, all the branches are equally responsible for contributing to the end goal. Many times, their contribution is not visible, but it is still there. For example your sales team could have closed the deal because your customer enjoyed a smooth and fast experience on your website, or because your HR department hired a very highly qualified sales manager who is able to train your entire sales team on the importance of customer satisfaction, or because your legal team was able to keep you safe from all the legal troubles and that's why there was extra cash which was later used in marketing and advertising, generating prospects for your sales team.

There can be many scenarios like this. All you have to remember is to understand the value of all your business branches. In the end, you want a business where everything is as strong as it can be.

Problem 6) I don't know much about my business environment

"This can make or break your business."

The understanding of the environment - political, economic, social, technological, and legal is very crucial for the success of a business. If you understand how these environmental factors are going to affect your business, you will be better prepared to handle any unexpected changes. You will understand more about the relevance, feasibility and profitability of your product in the market which is controlled by the external environment.

What Can Go Wrong While Setting Up Business Goals?

Businesses exist because they create value for the customers and in return, create value for themselves. Not the other way around. **You're not in the business because you want to create the value for yourselves.**
Sometimes confusions like this can lead to a completely wrong business goal setting.

Mistake 1) Sacrificing your long-term goals over short term goals

Short-term goals are more gratifying than the long-term goals. They provide fast visible results which blur your vision of the future. You become myopic in your thinking and are unable to think far ahead in time. You forget to see how these goals fit in your complete business picture of long-term survival and growth.

Many businesses have failed mainly because of this mistake. The present rosy picture of their businesses had stopped them from noticing the distorted future. You have to remember that even though the long-term goals are tougher and time-consuming to achieve, but in the end, they are more rewarding. Even more, your short-term goals should be linked to your long-term goals with more focus on the future.

Mistake 2) Setting up selfish goals

A business becomes successful when it becomes mutually beneficial for you and your customers.
You make money because your customer derives value and satisfaction from your products and services which help them in solving one of their problems. A business is like a give and take process. If you're focusing on just "participating" you will not be able to build a flourishing business.

Being selfish in the business is a sure path to failure.

You have to make sure that you are always thinking about your customers, and how you plan to serve them and make their lives better. When you take care of your customers, they will reward you with increased business sales and increased profits in return.

Mistake 3) Not having SMART goals

Your goals should always be specific, measurable, accurate, relevant and time-efficient. This makes sure that you are checking the performance of your business based on accurate goals. You need to have the right destination before you can plan your journey.

Mistake 4) Having wrong goals

The secret to setting up the correct goals is to always tie your goals to your customers.

If the end result is customer satisfaction, your business will thrive. If the end result is customer loyalty, your business will bloom. That's why it's important to keep your focus on your customers and build long running and profitable relationships with them.

Mistake 5) Unrealistic goals

I'm going to give you some real examples from my conversion with some of the business owners.

> Scenario 1
> Pooja - What do you have to say about your business?
> A - My idea is so unique. My company is going to be a billion-dollar company in the next five years.

> Scenario 2
> Pooja - What are you planning to achieve from this business?
> B - Can we sell these three products listed on every ten-year old ecommerce website, so we have some instant money to invest on my next idea?

> Scenario 3

Pooja - What's going on with your business?

C - I have started a website. Will I start making money by next month?

I'm going to disappoint you but none of these scenarios are realistic or even achievable goals (exclude some exceptions).

Scenario 1 - The success of an idea is dependent on more than just the idea itself. It depends on the execution of that idea.

Scenario 2 - Just making a website and adding a few products isn't enough to start making money through an ecommerce business.

Scenario 3 - If you enter a market with an undifferentiated product, there aren't many chances you'll make money soon.

Just like me, you must know many people who have started a business or just a website with great enthusiasm and then after a few months or years have abandoned everything. When you ask them what happened, they will say that the market was not right, there was not enough profit margin, there were too many competitors, clients were too demanding or something totally new.

Unfortunately, most of these issues were always present, even before the business was established. So, because of the poor understanding of the business as a whole or what types of business goals should be implemented, it leads to a stage of downfall.

Imagine working on everyone's favorite childhood painting - a house, a hill, a sun, and a tree. You can perfect the sun in the painting and not focus on other elements there. In a scenario like this, you're not going to get a perfect painting, you're just going to get a perfect sun in a not-so-good painting. But you can't become a successful painter if only one element of your painting is strong, but others are not.

Sometimes, you have to take your eyes off that sun and look at the picture as a whole, from a distance and see how they all fit together on one canvas. Same with your business. The moment you realize that your business is made up of so many pieces, you will see that any of those things can hurt your chances of success when not taken care of.

A perfect website with perfect marketing but bad financial management can fail, similarly a perfect product with a perfect website but bad customer management strategy can fail.

Everything needs to work in sync and to the best of their ability for a business to prosper.

References
12.https://www.newyorker.com/sports/sporting-scene/complexity-and-the-ten-thousand-hour-rule
13. https://wpforms.com/ecommerce-statistics/

CHAPTER 6

Failure to Lead and Manage Well

"To handle yourself, use your head; to handle others, use your heart." — *Eleanor Roosevelt*

The Story of Dissatisfaction

A long time ago when I was working for a company, I'd noticed what poor or non-existent leadership looks like. The employees were quitting the company at a rapid rate. I will say that during my time there I have seen people quit in less than a week. A few of them lasted for two to three months but nobody had lasted for a year.

Interviews took place every day because the positions were always vacant. This should have been a red flag for any kind of company. If you can't build a team that loves your company and your product the way you do, you're going to face a hard time bringing your idea to life. It doesn't imply that you should fire all those people who you think don't love your product. Love and respect are developed with the proper leadership. If you think your employees are not very passionate about your company, your idea or you, you'll need to work on your leadership skills instead of rehiring a different set of employees.

As in this story, the CEO of the company put the entire blame on the employees. She focused on the unreal part that those employees were not good employees instead of analyzing the root cause of the high employee turnover rate. One employee can be bad, two can be bad but if the majority of the employees are sharing the same viewpoint, then I think it's time for introspection.

There were a lot of negative reviews being shared about the company and the management on the reviewing websites like Glassdoor. Unfortunately, instead of listening to the issues raised by the former employees and working on fixing the problems, they'd kept discussing with their lawyers if they can sue those employees for raising fingers on the leadership. They even decided to buy some reviews so as to bury down the negative reviews, but the plan didn't work. Even if it would have worked, they could have improved their external image although the internal image would have remained the same - full of dissatisfaction and unhappiness.

It was a company where everything was screaming of bad leadership and ever worse management skills but only if somebody wanted to listen.

One time the CEO came to the office after her vacation, she banged her hands on the table and commanded that now we have to work triple what we were doing before.

That sounds really motivating! Doesn't it?

Do you think employees started working three times more? Of course, not!

The first thing that you can learn as a leader is that you're not working with robots but with emotional beings. The most important tool you will utilize for your business growth are your employees. You have to build their motivation and increase their productivity skills by being a better leader, not by giving commands. Those days of autocratic leadership style are gone. It's the age of partnerships where all your employees are your partners.

"People are working at your company because they are stuck with you" or "People are working at your company because they love it" are very different contexts. The first one shows you an example of bad leadership and the second one the real, good and effective leadership.

How is a Good Leader Different from a Bad Leader?

Have you ever heard that people don't change their jobs, they change their bosses? To an extent, we can all relate to this. We all have been there where we had to deal with a bad, unreasonable, unjust, incompetent, sexist, racist, homophobic or inefficient boss. Working for any such boss makes us so frustrated that we either end up quitting or reaching the edge where we think of nothing else but quitting. Please do not give your employee a reason to pour hot coffee on you out of built up frustration.

A long time ago, in one of my early jobs, I was reporting to this person who was a very strict workaholic. He would make everyone work very late hours. He was strict and assertive in a manner to get work done. Even though he was a terrible leader, he did one thing right and that was setting an example of himself before asking others to do so. He himself stayed late when he asked his team to stay late.

Now, let me tell you about my other boss from the same company. Unlike the first one, this one never led by an example. He'd expected everyone to stay in the office until night but he himself left the office at 5:00 PM sharp. Not just that, he was biased and preferred men over women. My reporting manager told me in my appraisal meeting that only two employees could be given excellent ratings and our sexist boss has decided to give it to two men who haven't even started working yet. She continued, "I know it's not right and shouldn't happen this way but there is nothing I can do."

Both cases are examples of bad leadership and managerial skills. In the first case, the discontent was just a little bit but in the second case, the discontent was multiplied. What do you think happened after that? I quit. Isn't that the story of many of us?

Only once in my life, I'd worked for a boss who was an actual team builder, a motivator, a nurturer and an inspirer. He was the first one to take responsibility when things went wrong and also, the first one to share credit with his team when amazing business results were achieved. He not only inspired all the team members to perform better, but he'd reduced the employee turnover rate drastically. Such is the power of a great leader!

From these cases, you can see that a bad leader leaves you demotivated and frustrated which hinders you from contributing 100% to your job. A good leader, on the other hand, knows how to bring the best out of you.

The Importance of a Great Leader

The importance of good and strong leadership lies in the fact that more than 50% of businesses fail after five years in the business.[14] Most of the time the reason for failure is not poor marketing and advertising but poor leadership skills.

Not just poor leadership, many times companies fail from a lack leadership. In a case like that, all the team members don't have any direction and feel lost.

Problems Arising Because of Poor Leadership Skills

- ## Low Company Morale

  Some leaders end up creating such a toxic environment that it becomes hard for anyone to thrive there. As a result, company productivity and morale go down. Not to mention employees' engagement which starts suffering heavily as well. Employees become unable to think out of the box or engage with others to figure out improved ways of solving the same problem.

  Once I was having a conversation with my friend who had worked in London. She told me how unhappy she was in the job as her boss was sucking the life out of her. She couldn't even tell her boss of her engagement because her boss didn't like anything like engagements and marriages that could distract her employees from work.

  Do you think such companies can ever reach the heights they are capable of? No!

  So often it happens that the problem doesn't lie in your product but in your leadership skills. You have to always remember that unhappy employees will not give their full potential. So, if you want to go big, the first thing you need to learn is that **your employees need more than just pay checks.**

- ## Reduced Productivity

  When your employees aren't motivated, inspired and empowered, they are not able to give their one hundred percent. This leads to reduced productivity which affects the growth of your business.

- Poor Team Management

  Great leaders help in building teams that work as one entity, trying to achieve the same common goal. Bad leaders,
  on the other hand, fail to understand the importance of
  a strong team and how the chemistry among those team
  members can affect the project output.

- Unclear Communication

  Before your team can start working on the projects they
  have been assigned, they need clear guidance, instructions
  and action plan. For this purpose, clear communication becomes an important trait of a good leader.

  In addition, you need to encourage two-way communication. You have to make sure that your employees feel comfortable when approaching you.

- Inability to Attract and Retain Good Talent

  You can attract and retain good talent, only if you have
  great leadership skills. A leader knows that humans are
  not robots. You can't feed another block of code in them
  to make their productivity go up two times or their motivation level go up three times or their love for your idea go
  up by ten times. Humans are emotional beings. They love
  when they are listened to, motivated and nurtured.

- Bad Vision Translation

  In all the companies I have worked with, there was one
  thing in common: no employee has any clue about the vision of the company or how the project they are working on
  is going to contribute to that vision.

  One company made it even worse when the vice president
  told the team in a meeting that the CEO wants to fill this

room up with the money. I was like "Wow! That's a great vision. Everyone in this room now feels super excited and motivated to increase their productivity so that they can fill this room up with the money for our CEO." These are the kinds of goals that sound good when you hear from drug cartels.

In simpler terms, the vision of a company is never to make money, it's higher than that. It's about the contribution to society and when you make your team aware of that, you will be able to unite them easily.

When employees are able to feel what you feel and see what you see in your idea, you won't need anything else to motivate them, and the success will become inevitable.

Lack of Transparency

If you want your team to contribute to the project, first they need to know everything about that project. Lack of transparency will keep them in the dark. If your team can't see the purpose of doing a particular task, they will not be able to contribute as they are supposed to. Enron was one such company.[15] Lack of transparency led to accounting fraud which ultimately led to the filing of bankruptcy.

Poor and Toxic Work Culture

Racism, sexism and nepotism: all of these lead to a toxic culture. How many times do we see how a leader ends up promoting someone with no skills or talent for some totally wrong reason? Not just that, sometimes leaders can have wrong expectations, unjust behavior, disrespectful attitude or they can be ignorant of their team members' needs.

Good leaders are above all that. They think of their team first before they think of themselves. As a result, the team feels they're being listened to which helps in increasing the satisfaction level.

- ## Poor Decision Making

  Many companies have failed because of the poor decision-making skills of top leaders. Decision making is an important task for any business leader. What is more important than the right decision-making is the ability to make that decision at the right time. Kodak, Best Buy and Blockbuster have failed for the same reason.

Many times, when I work with companies, they describe their business problems to me as poor marketing, inefficient advertising, not-so-great team, or something else. But what they all fail to analyze is their own image as a leader. Any kind of marketing and advertising can't bring the productivity of your team up, you are at your own here.

That's why a simple change such as improving your leadership style can save your business from failure.

Being a leader is like being a teacher. You teach your team members, you shape them, and you help them achieve success while continuing to be there whenever they need you.

What Makes Leadership Ineffective?

- ## Lack of Vision and Mission

  Vision and mission are more important than you think. Your vision is something which is going to unite all your employees by a common goal and will give them a proper direction to follow to achieve that goal.

  For that very reason, having the right vision which is very important in defining the character of a leader and in motivating the employees. If your vision is to earn a lot of money, this is not the kind of vision that can inspire your employees.

I have talked to many such business owners who ignore the importance of having a good vision and mission because they think it is obviously money and they even tell their employees the same.

"You have to work extra hard because I want to make extra money." This doesn't seem right. A vision needs to show the future goals of your company and these goals need to be beneficial for all including your employees, customers, stakeholders and most importantly, the environment.

Love for the environment is very important. If you don't care for your environment, you'll establish an image of a company which just thinks of itself. Your vision should be something that can equally inspire everyone who is associated with your project and not just you. If you start your business for a wrong reason, you will have trouble transferring your vision or the kind of emotions you have for your project to your employees. If employees are not inspired, you won't be able to reach your full potential.

- Lack of Accountability

Things don't always go right!
Mistakes happen.
Faulty actions are taken and executed.
But these mistakes are not the problem. The problem is how you handle those situations when things don't go as you've planned.

Do you schedule a meeting and shout at your employees, blaming them for not working hard enough? Or do you take accountability of those actions as their leader? The second option definitely seems tough, but this is the only right answer.

A good leader never takes credit but always takes the blame. I have worked with both kinds of leaders. The first one makes your employees frustrated, lose faith in you and your vision, while the second one sculpts you as a great leader. It shows that even if things go wrong, you will be there to support them, to show them the right path to achieve that goal.

- Lack of Focus

I had once worked with a business owner who wanted to see huge profits from his start-up in the first three months. He'd failed to realize that three months is not even enough time to create brand awareness about a totally new idea with a limited budget. Not able to see instant results, he'd started becoming distracted by other ideas.

He had wanted to experience instant gratification rather than long-term growth. For that reason, within two months of the project launch, he'd started losing his focus on his main project and started spending his time and energy on some other ineffective ideas. Suddenly, he wanted to restart his old and failed ecommerce idea. This thing kept going on for quite some time before returning back to his original project. But in this entire process, we lost a lot of valuable time and money.

Lack of focus generally emerges from the lack of vision. In the course of execution of your idea, you will get distracted a lot and you will start making a lot of changes without giving enough time for a plan to show results. Your attention might get diverted to a lot of similar ideas.

But you need to remember that nothing happens overnight.
No plan becomes successful in a day.
Just like a seed doesn't turn into a tree the next day after

sowing it. In a similar fashion, your idea takes time as well. Amazon was launched in 1994, almost twenty-seven years ago. They didn't become huge right after the launch.

So, don't rush. Don't lose your focus. Believe in your vision and your action plan. Wait for some time before you think of making any big change in your idea. Even if you might have unlimited wealth but your time is still limited. Spending your resources on useless things is not a good idea.

- Wrong Choice of Partners

When we start a project, we partner with other people because no project can be executed by just one person. Often times, we partner with our friends who can compensate for the skills that we don't have and sometimes with complete strangers. You may have a great idea of starting a restaurant in Prospect Park, Brooklyn but you might not have any restaurant experience. So, you might think of partnering with somebody who has a lot of experience in this area so that your vision and their experience can bring the desired results.

But when you do that, you have to make sure that you are partnering with the right partners. So many companies have split up and even failed because of the disagreements between the two. Not only will clashes bring your project to a stop, it also brings a lot of bad publicity to your project.

- Poor and Inadequate Management Skills

A great leader knows how to build a team who takes pride in their leader's vision and believe in it as their own. One simple rule to decide what kind of management skills you have is to learn how your team talks about you when you are not in the room. Do they talk about you with the same respect and love as they do in front of you? If the answer is yes, there is nothing much I can teach you about this because you have already mastered the art of managing people and building a team that loves you.

People skills are very crucial for the purpose of proper team building. Team building takes extra effort because you have to spend time to understand your employees and their needs, just like you try to understand your customers' needs. This will pay you back abundantly.

In addition to building a strong team, you also have to motivate that team when their spirits are down, show your pride in them when they perform good, and be there when they make mistakes. You have to invest in their training and start treating them as partners in your business' success.

- Lack of Authenticity and Transparency

We can achieve more if we are genuine and transparent to others. Nobody likes a company where there are many hush-hush meetings and you don't know what exactly is happening in those meetings. When there is transparency, your employees are aware of how their work is contributing to the project which makes them become more committed to the project.

When a team member doesn't know why they are doing something and how it is going to contribute to the final vision, they lose interest in their work because they are not able to see the importance of their work.

You have to start treating your employees as equals and start sharing things with honesty. By doing so, it will make them feel a part of the project, but it will also make them think of new and improved ways of doing the same things. They will become more productive as well as creative. You can't underestimate the power of that as you never know from where the next big idea is going to come from.

- Inability to Gain Love, Respect and Trust

Love, respect and trust - if you have all three as a leader, you are an exceptional leader. You're a leader who can inspire anyone and bring out the best in them. In case you have just one of the three or two of the three, then you have a long road to cover.

Trust plays an important role in making you a great leader because if your employees don't trust you, they won't trust in your vision or the action plan that you will share with them. Without trust, your employees will never be able to achieve their best and won't be able to put that toward the success of their project. Imagine what trust issues do to a relationship and the relationship between a leader and the follower is the same. It's very fragile.

You have to earn respect because you're a leader and you deserve a great deal of respect because of your vision, expertise, experience and the ability to lead people to the destination without ever letting them get entangled in any kind of storms.

You guide your team when they lose the path, you pick them up when they fall, and you give them motivation when they have none.

Love is needed because love is the answer to all. Isn't it? Actually, love is even above respect. I had once read that respect comes into play when there is no love left. Imagine having a team that not just respects you but loves you. Can you even think what wonders you can perform with a team like that?

- Being Hard to Work With

Being a boss is one thing but being hard to work with is another thing. The latter will reflect in your final result.

Are you open to hearing other people's opinions or do you shut them off because how would others know better than you? Do you welcome all ideas and feedback with open arms because you know that you still have so much to learn?

How do your employees feel when it comes to talking to you? Can they easily share their ideas and concerns with you, or do they keep their ideas mainly to themselves? How do your meetings go? Are you the one who talks the most or are your employees encouraged enough to contribute their views as well?

If you are hard to work with, you won't be able to build good and profitable business relationships. You might lose many good business partners, vendors and even employees because they will find it tough to work with you.

Once there was an IT head in one of my past companies who would not listen to anything his employees had to say and always said things like, " We don't do that here, we don't work that way here," or "What you are doing is wrong, do it my way." He even interfered with other departments' work like marketing and told the employees there that everything they were doing was wrong as this was not the way it happened twenty to thirty years ago when he had started his career. He would exclaim many times that we have no need for digital brand awareness campaigns because we never needed that twenty years ago.

What happens in situations like that is the junior employees will try for some time to show the importance of digital technology and how the world has changed in the last thirty years. That the world is doing many things that was not done in the past. But when faced with continuous resistance, the employee gives up.

It happens when management is not willing to listen to the other side. This should also be taken as a reminder that there is a big difference between senior employees and junior employees. When senior employees bring expertise and experience, young junior employees bring new perspectives. Therefore, both are equally as important.

How Your Organizational Structure and Management Style Can Affect Your Business' Growth

There's a concept in spirituality which says that whenever something goes wrong, the first thing we do is find fault in our external world. To put blame on somebody or something other than ourselves is the easiest way to protect our ego. But the very moment we look internally, we realize where the actual problem lies. It has always been there, but we just took longer than usual to identify it.

Organizational structure and management style are those two factors which we always forget to analyze when the performance of our businesses go down. We either blame the marketing team for its ineffective campaigns or we blame the current market situation and globalization for increasing the competition for local businesses or we find something else. In short, there is always something or someone to blame.

Just like our mental well-being, the secret to a healthy and prospering business also lies in the introspection. Sometimes it's good to look internally before blaming the external factors. This will help you to figure out what you are doing right and what you are not, what are the problem areas of your business and how can you improve them.

How Your Organizational Structure is Leading Your Business Toward Failure

Your organizational structure can hurt or promote your team's productivity. Simple things like how you set up your business, organize your departments and administer them can affect your business's long-term existence.

Every form of organizational structure comes with its own set of advantages and disadvantages and the best we can do is to capitalize on their benefits without adopting their faults.

We know bureaucratic organization structure is very rigid. Sometimes getting even a fruitful idea across to the right person becomes like climbing the steepest hill. Its rigidness hurts many employees' morale, their potential to achieve professional growth and their motivation level.

On the other hand, we know that entrepreneurial structure brings a lot of open communication, and flexibility. But after some time, as your team starts growing, entrepreneurial organizational structure becomes tough to maintain. Imagine one hundred employees having a discussion on how to implement a strategy! Most of them won't contribute and the meeting will mainly turn into a monologue. In case they all contribute, just think of all the confusion it will lead to. Remember the saying, "Too many cooks spoil the broth."

Here are some of the issues that inhibit a business from achieving its full potential:

1. Steep Hierarchy Level

The steeper the hierarchy gets, the tougher the communication becomes. The chain of command can be a little steep, but the chain of communication can't be. It's understandable that the top level of management can't give orders to the juniors directly as they don't have as detailed information as the manager directly responsible for managing that project. But this is not the reason to avoid having any kind of interaction with the junior employees in your company.

In addition to this, a steep hierarchy level can even lead to miscommunication or loss of information. Remember the telephone game or the Chinese whispers. Now, imagine a very important information is being passed from one level to another. It need not be just information from top to bottom, it can even be an innovative idea from bottom to top.

Not to forget that it can even make many employees feel disconnected from the overall mission of the business. As their professional world starts revolving more and more around their immediate bosses, they are not able to grasp a full understanding of what's going on in the entire organization and how their work is contributing to the organization and not just to their department.

2. Confused Entrepreneurial Structure

It's no surprise that in an entrepreneurial organization structure, we are generally wearing more than one hat. The team is quite small, and the responsibilities are shared among all. In a situation like that, with many overlapping functional areas and goals, job descriptions start becoming blurred. With that, even the goals a team member is required to achieve become blurred as well.

I have once worked for a start-up. Even though hired as a marketer, I was handling the responsibilities of various departments: PR, copywriting, marketing, sales, technical problem solving and even web design. When you wear many hats, it's expected that you are going to receive orders from various departments as well. This leads to just creating enormous amounts of confusion as all the departments have their own goals.

Sharing responsibilities in a start-up kind of structure is not bad, but you still have to make sure that your employees have well-defined job descriptions. Clearly defined job roles will eliminate any kind dilemma. It will help an employee better understand what they are supposed to achieve as a part of their job description.

3. Ineffective and Old Business Policies

Every business has a lot of documents related to policies, procedures and rules. We are always so busy with other work that we forget about these outdated documents. When these outdated documents are shared with the new employees, it leads to many problems.

4. Broken Information Flow

A successful organization will always have an effective two-way communication system where information can easily flow from one level to another. Many times, the information from the top management is not able to reach the junior employees and many times the suggestions and ideas by junior employees are not able to reach the top management. The end result: your employees feel detached from the organization's overall goals.

Not just the organizational structure but the management style can also affect your business goals of success and growth.

How Your Management Style is Leading Your Business to Failure

The role of management is a very critical one. They are not just responsible for managing the employees but also to make sure that the employees are productive and motivated. A good management style will make the productivity of your employees go up which means your revenues and profits go up as well.

There are various styles of management: authoritative, coercive, democratic, coaching or something else. The right and the most effective way of management is not adopting just one style but changing your style according to the situation.

Sometimes you have to be strict so they take their deadlines seriously and sometimes you have to be lenient so they can think creatively. Sometimes you want to be one of them but sometimes you want to be their leader. Sometimes you have to teach them with proper training and be open to learn from them as well.

In the end, there is no standard approach to a management style. You will be required to change your style according to your employees, business situation and time. The best you can do is not be too strict and also, don't be too lenient. Be like parents who adopt different ways to handle different situations so as to receive the right response from their kid.

References
14. https://www.fundera.com/blog/what-percentage-of-small-businesses-fail
15. https://www.investopedia.com/updates/enron-scandal-summary/

CHAPTER 7

Failing to Understand Customer Needs

"Walk with me for a while, my friend—you in my shoes, I in yours—and then let us talk." — Richelle E. Goodrich, Smile Anyway

The Story of "Being in Your Own Shoes."

In 2011, there once was a school in Pennsylvania. Even though this was one of the most successful schools, their decision-making wasn't so great. Their downfall started as they stopped listening to the students and started making decisions based on their understanding of the students.

One's needs and others' understanding of one's needs - these two are very different. It seems easy and very obvious when we think about what others are going to like but it doesn't work that way. Humans' needs are never constant, and they are also very complex.

As in this case, the school management kept investing in their infrastructure - something which was directly visible to parents and students, but they had stopped investing in good teachers who could have improved the quality of their service, education. They've always thought that students were not mature enough to know what is good for them in school and what is not.

But this is where they were wrong.

The two main mistakes in this case were:

1) Even if your customer is not an adult, always remember that they are way smarter than you think. Kids know exactly what they want, and they have the power of influencing their parents' decisions. In the example above, kids wanted good infrastructure, but they also wanted good teachers.

2) School management can impress parents with their fancy infrastructure, but students have to spend more time there than their parents. Consequently, paying more attention to the needs of students becomes way more important than any other investment. As in the case above, as the quality of education decreased, many students started switching to different schools.

Just getting students enrolled in the school is not the goal of any school, building a strong alumni community who love and adore your school is. And for that, you have to start listening to your customers (in this case, your students) and continue evolving your business.

There is one thing that I have heard a lot from people and I'm sure you must have as well. It is, "I love my school but only because I've made good friends there." Now, imagine your students saying to others, "I love my school because it is the best, just like what I had wanted." Isn't it better? It's definitely something to aim for.

The Mystery of Customer Behavior

Even though understanding customer behavior seems like a mystery, it is not. Customers need to know that they are heard, and their opinions are respected and acknowledged.

Today's customers need a little more from you than just your product. They want to see if you are just like them. They want you to stand for the right cause at the right time. As it reflects the kind of values you uphold and thus makes it easier for them to see you as a human being and not as a non-living business entity.

Even if your product is exactly what they are looking for, if you don't support a cause they are interested in, you won't be able to turn them into your customers. Customers these days are becoming more and more concerned for mother earth. As a consequence, they are not going to support any product which harms the environment. So, think for a second what kind of values you want your business to have.

Build a brand image that matches your customers' values and stick to it. Don't hesitate to show your support to those who are in need of it. Many businesses have suffered a backlash and were boycotted because they didn't stand for a cause when they were supposed to, or one of their team members made racist remarks, or the business wasn't respectful to every customer who has visited them.

This was the reason why Starbucks had to shut down their stores for a day so they can teach their team what is right and how to stand for what is right.[16] If they would not have done that, even though how addicting their coffee is, many would have easily sacrificed their products over another brand's coffee just because the other company seemed more sensitive to people's emotional needs.

I myself know many people who avoid going to a few stores because they either failed to support the black lives matter cause, weren't environmentally friendly, said something racist, mistreating their workers or had done something which didn't reflect the values the customers could have identified with.

The New Definition of Customer Behavior

Customer behavior is not just defined by what your customers want but also by what they believe in.

They may want a good quality camera but not from every company. Only from a company which matches their mindset or their values.

Understanding Customer Behavior

If you want to understand their needs, you have to do research- primary and secondary both. You can interview them, notice their behavior, mystery shop, conduct surveys, organize focus groups, do alpha and beta testing, and a lot more.

In addition to that, you can also use data from secondary sources and analyze that. Remember primary and secondary research work in tandem. You can't just depend on the secondary research. You will be needing both and there is no way out of it.

There are many business owners who make the mistake of just doing the secondary research - reading news articles, checking out other companies' research as it's easy and cheap but that's not enough. You need more than that. You need to be in touch with the potential customers who you want to start buying your products.

This doesn't imply you have to go talk to each and every one of them but at least a set of people who can represent your entire target audience very well. For that, we invest in primary research.

Research is just the starting point. You will also be required to start collecting the feedback of your customers at every stage, so you know that they have not developed any discontent for your products. Speaking about feedback reminds me of an ecommerce company where customers kept quitting the cart after going to the product page. The business owner was supposed to add a small survey or give a page to contact them or share their feedback so they know exactly what is happening and why the customers were leaving the website after reaching the checkout page. But the business owner completely ignored the importance of that. He kept guessing, putting pressure on his team to perform better but never spent any time asking the people who were facing the issue - the customers.

In another similar example, there once was a company which launched an app, but the app was full of technical issues. The management instead of fixing those issues, asked the marketing team to force the customers to buy the product instead of fixing all the technical glitches. First, marketing is not magic. Second, customers are way smarter than you think. If you know these two things, you will know that the approach the management followed couldn't bring any positive outcome for them.

Marketing can neither sell a broken product nor can it mend a broken heart.

Ethical marketing is the only way of marketing. By doing that, you don't disguise the faults of your products, but instead you try to fix them. When you do that, the results are long-lasting.

As was previously stated, marketing is not the solution for broken or poorly designed products. Listening to your customers and introducing those changes in your products is.

The Secret of Business Growth

Let's consider a simple scenario. There is Mr. Alex Montli who has a problem with dry hair and is looking for a shampoo to solve the issue. Which option, out of the following, do you think he should choose?

Product 1 = Shampoo for smoothing dry hair
Product 2 = Shampoo for thick hair
Product 3 = Shampoo for thin hair
Product 4 = Shampoo for colored hair
Product 5 = Shampoo for curly hair
Product 6 = Shampoo for gray hair
Product 7 = Shampoo for oily hair
Product 8 = Shampoo for normal hair
Product 9 = Shampoo for long hair
Product 10 = Shampoo for damaged hair
Product 11 = Shampoo for dogs

The answer is product 1.

Let's say that product 1 is not available on the market and he needs something urgently. What's he going to pick now? Maybe product 8 or product 10.

If you want business growth, you are going to offer the right product to the right customer which means you are going to sell product 1 to Mr. Montli. If not, you can offer an alternative like product 8 or 10. On the other hand, if you really want to piss off your customer and want to be completely ignored by him, you're going to offer any other product to him.

Imagine how would you feel if you suddenly start seeing ads for shampoo for an oily scalp all over the internet, even though you have a dry hair problem. Maybe in the beginning, you will take it lightly. Maybe you will make fun of them a little for targeting the wrong audience and wasting their marketing budget. But after some time, you will be frustrated at that company for targeting an irrelevant product to you and you might even mark their ads as spam.

Nine Mistakes to Avoid

- Treating Customer Needs as Fixed

Customer needs are never the same. They change over time, when the environment around them changes or the life stage of your customer changes.

A couple without kids will not mind a small apartment in the city but as their family grows, they will prefer a bigger home, maybe in the suburbs. This is an example of changing needs according to their life stage.

Let's take another example, the younger generation will prefer a platform for the easy sharing of videos like TikTok rather than Facebook because their needs are different.

Here's one more scenario for you. Your customer moves to Europe from the US. They will be now required to make different product choices as they will start incorporating various parts of European culture in their day to day lives consciously or unconsciously. This shows the changing needs of customers based on the change in location.

Customers can even become health conscious after binging on desserts for most of their lives. In this case, the preferences and attitudes of the customers have changed as they have adopted a new way of living. Similarly, customers won't care about laundromat service as much when living in Louisville as they will care about when they are in New York City. Similarly, a high-heel lover can pretty easily switch to comfortable shoes as they get older, or are required to walk a lot, or suffer from a knee problem.

Interestingly, needs can also change based on emotions

or perceptions. Customers can stop buying their favorite products from a brand because the company said something that they don't agree with.

In short, customer needs are changing with every moment.

Everything around your customers is shaping those needs and wants. We can't stop this change from happening, but we can listen. That way we are better prepared to help them make the transition with our products whenever they are ready.

- Targeting Everyone

This is another big issue that hinders the business growth. Many business owners fail to understand that **targeting everyone is like targeting nobody.** Blinded by the misconception that by targeting everyone, they can increase the reach of their products and sell more, instead they end up losing their limited budget in inefficiency. This is also something very common with new entrepreneurs. I can't count how many times the answer to the question, "Who is your target audience?" was as broad as:
All the women in the USA.
All the people living in Brooklyn.
Everyone who is 20+ years old.
Everyone who has a job.

The numerous combinations that can be made based on people's culture, religion, life choices, values, attitudes, interests and more, make a broad target audience very fruitless.

Even if we are able to categorize all these people based on a few factors like their location, gender and age, they will still remain very different from each other. Customers in Portland are very different from the customers in New York and the customers in New York are very different from the customers in Los Angeles.

Eventually, it's important that instead of targeting all and depleting the business budget on your poor choices, you should start by finding the right set of potential customers. You should look for your niche: all those people who will love your product because their needs and your product benefits match. This way you will use your budget more efficiently.

When your business starts growing and you have more money coming in from your profits, then you can think of expanding your audience by doing proper market research and following a proper expansion strategy.

- Targeting Just on the Basis of Demographics

Take a moment to think about yourself. Who are you? Are you just a thirty to forty- year old single woman living in New York City? Or are you more than that? Do you think these words – thirty to forty-year old, single woman, living in New York capture the entire essence of who you are? Are these words enough to make you a good audience for many products? Definitely not.

Let's try to further define you. In addition to those general details about you, you don't like makeup and you love books. This statement has just excluded you from the customer market for beauty products. Can any kind of book authors target you for selling their books? No again.

Let's dig deeper. You don't like fiction books, you like non-fiction ones. This statement shows that not all the authors, publishing houses and booksellers can target you because you like to read a specific genre. This list of knowing and understanding you will keep going on until we hit the very atom of your existence. I understand that's not feasible, but we should try to reach a stage where our potential customer base is just perfect in size for us - not too big and not too little.

And when it comes to segmenting and targeting, remember demographics is just one way of segmenting your customers. You can try psychographics segmentation, and interest and intent-based segmentation as well. It's much better if you segment based on all those factors combined rather than just one.

- Ignoring Customer's Feedback

Most of the time small businesses don't show much interest in gathering their customers' feedback and if they do, they completely don't act on the gathered insights. There was one such company where whenever any feedback came from the customer, it was ignored because according to them, "Those particular customers don't fall within the our target audience set, so it doesn't matter much what they are saying" or their other response will be, "Can we exclude this set from our targeted audience as they don't seem to fall in the category of people we want to target?"

It's obvious, customers of that company were shouting every day what things they don't like about the product, and why or how it can be improved, but nobody was willing to listen to them. Their voices were subdued. Here's what it led to:

1. The problems that were making that product unpopular remained until the company existed. A product which could have been easily upgraded to a better version, gained competitive advantage and increased the customer satisfaction, was never improved and continued being sold as is.

2. Downfall of the product happened because they'd underestimated the power of the customers. Most of them were talking about the same issue. Even if they didn't fall in the

target category (let's assume that just for a moment), they had still pointed out the same problems. When more than one customer says the same thing, you need to start paying attention to that.

- Not Aligning Your Goals with Your Customers' Needs

So many times, business owners become obsessed with their own needs that they forget to see that a business is run properly when the needs of customers are taken care of.

A business becomes successful when it is able to satisfy the needs of its customers in a profitable way.

For this purpose, you have to start aligning your goals with your customers' needs. If you want to make your business profitable, don't think of earring profits by cheating or misleading your customers. On the other hand, make your product their dream product.

If they say I want a fast product because it saves me time, don't sell your product and label it as the fast one but actually work on your product to make it fast for them. This way your customers will feel delighted which will soon turn them into your loyal customers. And that my friend, is the secret of a successful profitable business - long-term relationships and loyalty.

- Not Interacting Enough with Customers

While a few businesses are ignoring the customers' feedback, a few others are not even interacting with the customers. You don't just research about your customers in the very beginning of your project and then forget about them, you have to continuously learn from them. If you stop doing that, your product will never evolve with the changing time and then your competitors will gain a competitive edge on you.

You have to interact with your customers continuously, not just once a year or once a month. The faster you learn how their needs are transforming, the faster you will be able to implement those changes in your products and can beat up your competition. You won't just remain a market leader in your field but in addition, your customers are not going to leave you.

We always talk about competition and how easily others enter your industry and become your competitors, but the biggest threat comes from how easily your customers can switch to another brand's products. If you are listening to your customers, then you don't have to worry about either of those two threats.

- ## Not Willing to Understand What a Customer Wants

Understanding what a customer wants is not that tough. It all starts with listening and understanding why they want this change. In most cases, the target audience is very different from the CEO or the management of the company. So, as a CEO, you can't guess exactly what your customers are looking for.

A working mom might prefer those products which can save her more time so she can easily balance her work and home life. Unless and until you are a working mom, you can't exactly say what they want. That's why we have to talk to them, have an open conversation, learn about what difficulties they are having and if there's any way your product can solve those problems.

If you want to understand your customers, you have to go to them. There is nobody else who can tell you what they want - neither you nor me because we are not living their lives.

Creating the Product from Your Point of View

There was a guy who was once obsessed with luxury products and that's what he did with his product as well. He tried to give a luxury twist to his product which was targeting low-middle income families. But he had forgot, for that audience set, luxury is not important as much as the real benefits of the products. They didn't care if the fabric of the purse was imported from France and that's why the price is higher. They cared about the quality and the affordability. They didn't care if the people working in the company loved luxury and knew a lot about it. They'd remained focused on a good bargain for their money.

This target group doesn't care if the services are going to be by an expert from France or England, they care if the services are going to fit the budget that they have allocated to this particular need of theirs and is going to give them the lowest post-purchase dissonance.

Post-purchase dissonance is when the customers regret the product that they have just bought.

That's why, you should always make sure that when you start working on your idea that you don't get distracted by your own needs and desires. You are not designing a product for yourself. You are not your target audience (except less than 1% cases where you can be). At every step, analyze if the product matches your customers' requirements or not.

Failure to Understand Your Market

Businesses fail when we don't understand our customers, they also fail when we don't understand our market. If you are trying to open a restaurant in a place where the majority of people are the practitioners of Judaism faith, then you cannot make a non-Kosher restaurant and still hope to gain popularity. Or if the majority of the people in your ideal business neighborhood are Italians, then opening a Russian grocery store there is not going to bring much business to you.

As a result, you should not just try to understand your customers, but also the market and make sure that the targeted market has the customers that you need. As it's not always easy to open a business in any location we want. Sometimes we have to figure out a business as per the location which is more convenient to us. A dentistry business in New York City, Brooklyn or Queens is not going to be the same as the market is very different in each of these locations.

In the end, the golden rule here is to stop assuming what your customers are going to like and what they won't. Instead, start putting yourself in their shoes to familiarize yourself with their needs and wants. That way you will never go wrong.

References
16.https://www.npr.org/sections/thetwo-way/2018/05/29/615119351/starbucks-closes-more-than-8-000-stores-today-for-racial-bias-training

CHAPTER 8

Running a One Man Show

"A star that helps another shine doesn't have to work twice as hard to light up the sky." — *Matshona Dhliwayo*

The Story of a Man with Multiple Jobs

There was once a start-up in San Francisco which provided online legal consulting. The business started off slow but received some clients eventually. Then it started becoming slow again. Soon after that, it failed to attract more clients and died.

Let us try to understand why it happened and if anything could have been done differently to save it.

This online consulting business was started by Mr. Edgar Johnson. He had many years of expertise in the field of law (but definitely not in the area of running a business). He'd decided to use his expertise to help more people which led him to start his company.

When he didn't get any clients even after one year, he had decided to start doing some marketing. But unwilling to hire a marketer or outsource the work to a marketing agency, he tried to do everything by himself. Now, he was doing the jobs of two people. His attention was divided. In his job as a marketer, he had no expertise and he had damaged the brand building process rather than strengthening it. In his other job as a legal consultant, he hadn't gained enough time to sharpen his skills as he was doing earlier.

Then, he decided to create some ads by himself and started advertising digitally. Of course, ads were mainly ignored as he didn't have any experience in the field of creative copywriting. A creative ad creation process involves a minimum of three professionals – a market research expert, copywriter and creative director. He was handling at least three jobs now.

He'd gained a few clients through word of mouth marketing but now he was also doing administrative tasks, in addition to the other tasks. Setting up appointments, documenting everything and answering phone calls and a lot more. He got a few other calls from potential clients, but he was not able to convert them. Instead of hiring a sales professional, he tried to do a lot by himself. Soon, it became a business with ineffective marketing, advertising, poor sales, and a bad client success program. Without any employees to share the load, Mr. Johnson started feeling burnt out as he tried to juggle everything by himself before succumbing to the inability to manage everything by himself and accepting the failure.

How many people around you have tried their hands at starting a business but failed? I am sure you know at least one person. Now, you can better tell what happened in most of those cases.

Jack of All, Master of None.

It's very tempting to do everything by yourself irrespective of your experience and expertise in any of those areas. You become influenced by the thought of being able to save a lot of money by not hiring professionals or working with other business partners, but it harms you in the long run. First, you don't get the professional help in the areas where you need plus you don't get enough time to practice or do what you love the most.

Imagine if you had implemented the professional marketing strategy right from the beginning, you would be able to build a lot of brand and customer equity that nobody could take away from you, even after you stopped marketing. But when you try to do it yourself, without any experience in this field, you'd also waste the marketing budget without seeing any results.

Additionally, without any experience, many things can go wrong which could affect your brand reputation. In a case like that, when you hire a marketing agency, they will be required to not just do the regular marketing services but also to fix your image which has been tarnished. This will delay their results and will increase your marketing budget.

I know you're thinking that you won't make any mistakes that will tarnish your brand image, but it happens a lot. One wrong social media post, wrong website link with another website, wrong image presenting to the audience, and many other things can damage your brand image considerably. I have worked with many businesses whose websites were either blacklisted or were put into totally different categories because of whatever they were doing before they'd partnered with me.

Sometimes, it can be inaction rather than just bad action that can affect your image. Ms. Tina Jones had to suffer a lot of backlash on her business' social media sites for her inability to share her views and take a side on a time when big things were happening in her city. As soon as she approached us with her problem, we started working on humanizing her business and building an improved brand image. This crucial step made her business' followers calm down but also respect her business more for doing the right thing at the right time.

You need to accept that you can't do everything by yourself. There is a reason why companies have employees. Yes, we understand you're just starting out and don't have enough budget. But you don't have to cut costs in all those areas which are important for business growth.

If you want to be big, you have to start behaving big. Starting days of a business are more of an investment rather than profit-making. You might not feel right when you will see money being debited from your account (without any credit coming in) but you are going to reap the benefits of your investments very soon.

Trying to Do Everything by Yourself

Many businesses fail because the founders don't realize that they are going to be more than just the founder or the owner of that business. You will be required to wear many hats. You have to be a leader. You have to motivate, inspire and engage with your employees. You have to build a strong team. You have to manage employees' expectations. Building a team is a huge task. This task can't be delegated to someone else. You're the leader of your business and you have to behave like a leader for your employees.

You have to be a leader who is loved, respected and trusted.

Then, your second role will be related to client success and relationship building. You will be required to hire an expert salesperson who can do it on your behalf and present a pretty picture of your brand to your clients. Many business owners try to do it by themselves but I strongly believe that if you don't have the personality of a sales person, you have to either practice hard and master it, or you can hire somebody else to do it on your behalf. Many deals fall through at this stage rather than at any other. Getting leads is the first step but converting those leads into satisfied customers is one of the most important and most challenging tasks of a business.

You also have to work for the benefits of the society, in general. You will be required to keep your stakeholders and partners happy, and make sure that your business policies don't clash with any government rules. Not to mention, you will be required to manage crises like an expert.

There are various other jobs that you need to do as a business owner. However, doing so much by yourself can be very exhausting. Sometimes, it can make you lose focus of your vision. You may find yourself distracted by many related and unrelated ideas. You may think that instead of a restaurant, I should open a bakery, or instead of a dress store, I should sell shoes, or instead of offering advertising services, I should become an influencer, but not getting lost in all these new ideas coming and leaving your mind is what's going to help you build a successful business. Focusing only on the idea that you've started will help you from giving up way too early.

Ruling Out Professional Help

We can't pretend to be a doctor and treat ourselves. Similarly, we can't wear the hat of an orthodontist, a reporter, a journalist, a chef, an accountant, a lawyer, a marketer, a copywriter, a creative designer or some other professional as and when we want. The reason being all these lines require proper knowledge of the industry and a lot of practicing to master the field. To quote Malcolm Gladwell again, at least 10,000 hours of practice. Many times, we are not able to see the complexity of a profession but it's still there.

There have been many cases where business owners posted something wrong on their social media channels and ended up hurting their business rather than building it.

Let me ask you this, how many people do you know who are getting leads through their social media? Not many. As social media involves more than just posting there and experts know that. People write their own ad lines these days but let's not forget why Mad Men became so popular. They know the secrets of advertising. Their ad copies are catchy, memorable, and nostalgic. How would you rate most of the ad copies being shown on online channels these days? Are they catchy, memorable and nostalgic? Do you remember any recent ad that you loved and can't forget? Not because 92% of Americans ignore at least one type of ad. Online ads are ignored by 82% of Americans.[17]

If you have a desire to succeed, you should know that you cannot rule out professional help. They have years of experience in all those fields that fall out of your expertise. They know what works and what doesn't. Consider all this as an investment in building a strong brand.

Not Having the Right Experience and Industry Knowledge

Establishing a business without any experience and industry knowledge is like playing basketball as a novice with Michael Jordan. Doesn't seem like the right move, right?

Let's say you are still adamant to do it. What will be the possible result? You will be out of the game as soon as you start.

Let's say everything favored you that day and you were able to defeat Jordan. Do you think you will still continue to defeat him match after match? No! You have to let go of your pride here and start thinking rationally. There won't be a day when you will become the basketball legend without any experience and skills unless you have some magical powers that I am not aware of. In the latter case, this book might not be very useful to you.

The rules of basketball apply to the business world as well. You can't enter it if you don't have the right experience combined with the right skills. If you want to win big and are planning to last longer than a few years, you have to come prepared. Always keep in mind that you're not going to compete with the beginners, you're going to compete with the masters.

The golden rule to guide you is, "Always treat your competitors smarter than you are." This way it will help you in figuring out the most effective ways of improving your performance and your business strategies. When you're ready to enter the battlefield of business, make sure you are armed with the two most important tools for business survival: industry experience and business knowledge.

Do you have the right experience to start your dream business?

People become experts only after many years of practice in their field. From Bill Gates to The Beatles, they all have spent countless hours mastering their art before they've became a huge success.

In addition to practice, there are a few more things that you have to pay attention to:

1. Mistaking Your Hobby for Your Business Idea

Mr. Jack Miller is a great baker. Everyone compliments his baking all the time. Motivated by all the compliments that he has gathered in his lifetime he finally decides to start his own baking business.

Is he doing anything wrong?

It depends on what kind of a business plan he has. If he doesn't have business knowledge and is not taking help from other business professionals, then he's making the mistake of confusing his hobby as his business idea. Hobbies can't always successfully translate into businesses.

Sometimes they are just undifferentiated hobbies just

like what many others have but we forget to see that in our entrepreneurial rush of excitement.

How many bakers, writers, knitters, photographers, painters, musicians or dancers do you know? Do you think they all can run a successful business? If not, why do you think so?

Similarly, Mr. Miller can be a great baker, but successful businesses need more than just skills. Setting up and running a business requires valuable industry experience.

This is one of the critical reasons why many small businesses fail. I am sure you must have seen at least one restaurant, cafe, or juice bar in your neighborhood which once existed but is now closed. Living in Brooklyn, I am surrounded with such businesses. If I can go back in time, I would hand out this book to them and let them know that they are not ready for a business yet. Hobbies can be deceptive. I have many hobbies. I read, cook, and make crafts with different kinds of materials, but I know not all those hobbies are going to turn into great business ideas.

2. Incomplete Industry Experience

Ms. Sarah Anderson worked as a web designer in the cosmetics industry for over ten years. Interestingly, she even has 10,000 hours of work experience. With that thought in her mind, she decided to launch her own cosmetics company.

Is anything wrong with that?
Thinking incomplete knowledge of the industry presents a fuller picture.

Running a cosmetics business needs more knowledge

than her limited exposure to the industry as a web designer. She needs to know about how to procure raw materials, how to manage the supply chain, how to satisfy the needs of the beauty buyers and many other similar things. She doesn't have any experience in those areas. Even though she has completed her 10,000 hours of practice, she has not earned the equivalent number of relevant hours needed for that business idea yet.

As a marketer, I have worked in the beauty industry, but I am not there yet where I can think of starting a beauty company.

How much experience do you have in your industry? Before I'd started my marketing and advertising agency, Bizadmark in New York, I made sure I'd have a minimum of 10,000 hours of relevant experience.

Do you have the right skills to start your dream business?

It's very simple. If you want to run a hospital, you need to know about running hospitals. If you want to start a school, you need to know about running schools. If you want to start a beauty company, you need to know how to run a beauty company (and not just cosmetics). The more you know about your industry, the more equipped you will become in understanding the needs of your customer and satisfying the same with your product.

Don't forget that you can only sell a thing that you have proficiency in.
Will you go to a dentist whose teeth are all messed up? Why not? Because you will expect that if they are selling us healthy teeth, their own teeth need to be a proof of their

beliefs and claims. It goes the same for every industry. You have to show your audience that you have the skills otherwise you won't be able to attract and retain them.

How to Ensure the Success of Your Business

- Develop Your Skills

Learn as much as you can. Become a part of that industry. If you want to have a web designing company, work in a web designing company for a few years. If you want to own a restaurant, work in a restaurant for some time.

When I say develop your skills, I don't mean related to every business area of that industry. This is not very realistic. I mean, the field of your expertise in that industry. If you are good at strategic thinking, keep working on that. Think of ways you can come up with better strategies. If you're good at client relationship building, then learn what more can you do and how can you keep different kinds of clients happy. If you're a great software developer, then don't stop programming. Learn what else is new in the market, learn those skills and apply them in your business.

The best gift you can give to yourself is to invest in yourself.
You have to grow as your business grows.

- Practice Until You're an Expert

Practice for enough time before you decide to run your own business. Your business idea can wait but don't enter a market without enough expertise and experience. If you enter the market, way too soon, you will lose your resources and will be out of the business.

Always remember there are many people who are doing something similar to you or are working on an idea similar to yours. While you are launching a project without enough knowledge, they can see your faults and weaknesses and can use that to their advantage. This will harm your position in the market and will establish your competitor's product as the leading one.

Don't confuse the skill that you are selling with the business knowledge. If you are planning to open a bakery, you won't just need to be a good baker, you also need to have a good business mindset. You can survive the industry if you have the latter, but you can't go much further in the other case. Many expert programmers tried to establish their own website businesses in the past few years without much luck because they have the expertise to design a good website but they don't have the business knowledge of how to get leads and then convert them into happy clients which is way more important for running a business.

It might sound slightly overwhelming, but if running businesses was so easy, everyone would be a successful business owner.

- ## Surround Yourself with Experts

Talk to others who run similar businesses. Learn more from them. Learn about their business journeys, the kind of challenges they have faced and the strategy they'd used to overcome them.

When you hear other experts share their experiences, your brain works better as it forces you to think of various scenarios and possibilities that you haven't thought of so far. Listen to podcasts or read books about various business journeys. Make it a part of your everyday life.

- ## Don't Do Everything Yourself

  It does sound tempting to do everything by yourself and save some money. But if you want long term growth, this is not the right way. If you're good at managing a hospitality business, then just focus on that. Don't try to wear many hats at the same time. Let others handle the rest.

  You don't have to be a copywriter, a marketer, a web developer, a PR professional, an influencer, an HR professional, and an accountant all at once. Let experts from other fields handle the rest so you can continue getting better at your core skill set.

Keep increasing your business and industry knowledge. Never stop. The goal is not to practice for some particular number of hours and then stop altogether. The goal is to continue getting that number of your practice hours higher and higher. Focus on your area of strength. If you lack management skills, build your own expert management team. If you lack marketing skills, hire a marketing agency.

If you have a great idea, let nothing stop you from bringing it to life.

Ignoring Signs of Burnout

Above all, you should keep an eye on any signs of feeling burnt out. If you think you're overburdened with your work, you can't do it all, hire a professional and delegate some work. When we share the load, we are able to finish that work much faster.

Build your employee team, hire assistants and interns, delegate as much work as you can so you can concentrate on the task which needs your focus the most. Those tasks that can't be delegated to others will need your visionary thinking.

In the long run, these costs will seem unnecessary. You may feel like you can be your own assistant, receptionist, and book-keeper, but it is not sustainable for long-term growth.

When we start a business, we feel this urge to have control over every aspect of it. We want to be involved everywhere, to keep an eye on everything. Sometimes we have to let go of this control issue and let professionals handle it. We should be there to guide them, but the professionals know what they are doing. If you have hired a marketer, you don't have to tell the person how to work, you can communicate where you want your business to go and the marketer can decide how to get there, whether your goals are realistic or not, what strategy to use and how to implement that strategy. Doesn't that remove a hell of a burden from your shoulders?

Remember you have a limited supply of resources which includes your time.

References

17.https://www.businesswire.com/news/home/20140211005607/en/Goo-Study-Ignore-Online-Ads

CHAPTER 9

Failure to Adapt with Changing Time

"The Only Thing That Is Constant Is Change." -Heraclitus

The Story of Isolation

This is the story of Mr. Keith Brown who ran a resort in the beautiful countryside of Washington. When he called Bizadmark, my company, to discuss his current problems, I was absolutely surprised to learn that he was still living in the era before the internet became huge. He told me that he wants to bring more customers to his resort. Currently, he is just relying on word of mouth marketing, but it doesn't always bring new customers.

During my conversation with him, he said he was going to the post office to drop off the direct mail to his former customers. I was again surprised as the world has already moved on from direct mail to emails and newsletters. He continued that the internet services are pretty bad in his city and that's why he doesn't have anything digital going on. Even his website was a website built when the internet just came out. Bad user interface and design. No way to contact anyone or block dates. The website experience was very bad.

On top of that, there was no marketing. He'd just relied on his old customers to come back but how often does that happen? There are always new places to explore. So, the number of repeat customers for non-business-related travel is not as high as we think.

Many customers shared bad reviews on the internet, but he never did anything to deal with them. Shockingly, he didn't even know there were reviews about his business. Now, imagine he was sending direct mail to all those unhappy customers as well who gave him bad reviews and he never acted upon those. How frustrating would it be for those customers to receive communication from a company that ignored their feedback?

In a way, he hasn't adapted to the changing technology. He has lost a lot of customers because of that. Even worse, his image has been stained as well with all the bad reviews he'd received which he had ignored unknowingly. At a stage like that, he not only needs marketing, but he also has to work on building his image as well as his resort's.

And yes, there were many other resorts in that area. Even though they had bad internet connection, they've all partnered with other marketing agencies. Now, he was also miserably lagging behind in the competition.

Change is a Way of Survival

Even though change is an important part of growth, we still face a hard time liking it. We try to resist it for as long as we can before giving up. Not just in our personal lives, but even in our professional lives we're faced with the same problem. We get so comfortable executing our businesses the way we have been doing that we reject anything new.

We are deluged with many questions when we think about

something new (and scary). "Why would I want to change an existing effective product? It can backfire. It can affect the profits I am currently making." Or "What about the time involved in training everyone to accept this change? I am going to lose so many valuable hours which will bring the sales down and I can't afford that." Or "I doubt this change is ever going to be accepted by anyone. This is unimaginable and I can't waste my resources on it."

We love being in our comfort zones but nothing big has ever been achieved from there.

What if Microsoft, Google and Apple would have had the same questions and would have continued selling the same old product they'd first created? What if most of the companies we love now have not adapted with time and continued doing their business the same old way they had before?

Then, you would not have the comfort of ordering your groceries online, or almost everything from anywhere. You wouldn't be able to get a taxi whenever and wherever you want. You wouldn't be able to book an Airbnb in the middle of nowhere where no hotels are available. You wouldn't be using your laptop sitting on a couch while talking to your friends but will be sitting next to a giant machine punching codes in it and waiting for hours to get a response.

We forget many times, but changes are not threatening as they are the only way to move forward. As a business owner when we adapt to that change, we are contributing to that progressiveness. But can adapting with time lead to business growth? I will say it can help you survive the transition time, but business growth will not come from this. Instead it will come when you lead the change.

Roadblocks to Adapting to Changes

- ## Poor Market Research

One of the most important factors that stops us from a change is poor market research. It's solely because of market research that only a few businesses are able to stay in the market for so long while others are being wiped out. Market research provides information about what new changes your competitors have made which you should too, before it's too late.

In addition, it helps you understand your customers in a better way. Your customers are always changing and so are their values, perceptions and needs. Having up-to-date knowledge about them will help you in satisfying their needs as well as delighting them.

Lastly, market research helps you understand the environment you're operating in which is very important for the proper function of your business. It prepares you when there are sudden changes in the laws that affect your business (like privacy laws, environment protection laws, advertising laws etc), or when your target audience changes (e.g. the population in your city getting old, or becoming a popular spot for tech residents) or when there are changes in the economy (e.g. more foreign investment is allowed which will increase more competition for you).

- ## Confusing Opportunities with Threats

I have said this earlier and I will say it again that o**pportunities and threats are different sides of the same coin.**

You can either see a change as a threat or you can see it as an opportunity. Interestingly, when you start seeing changing times as a threat, you will start directing your business toward stagnation and failure; but when you do the opposite, you will be steering your business toward business growth which is more than just business survival.

Let me tell you a story. Once there was Mr. Joe Tyrone who lived in my neighborhood and ran a packaging company. After successfully being in the business for many years, he finally had to shut it down recently. The reason being that with changing times, competition increased in his industry. And with that there were not just local competitors, but there were also global competitors like China. Whatever his company was doing, China was doing the same job but at a cheaper and faster rate with the help of advanced technology.

The question now is was there anything he could have done differently to face such challenging times like that? The answer is definitely yes. First, he should have adapted to the changing times and transformed his business from being a brick and mortar company to a digital business. Without any digital presence, he was just dependent on a few clients who worked with him. But how long can they stay loyal? A little market research could have helped him in understanding the scenario a little better.

Another company that considered change as a threat was Kodak.

Can you believe that they had actually developed a digital camera in the year 1975? Now you must be wondering why you've never came to know about it. Because it was never launched. They let the product die because they were scared that their innovative digital camera was going to cannibalize their other products like their photographic film. What they'd failed to see at that time was that they couldn't have stopped change by not launching their product. They didn't launch but their competitors did. The result was that they finally filed for bankruptcy in the year of 2012. Let that not be a story of your business.[18]

Let's take another example. Do you know that Xerox is the

company who developed the first computer? You must be wondering why we don't see any Xerox computers in the market then. Xerox was able to build a product which would soon become very popular but they didn't know how to capitalize on the market. Apple launched the first computer but the GUI and mouse that they used were actually built by Xerox scientists.

Why was Xerox not able to build a successful company like Apple even after being the ones to innovate the first computer? They couldn't see beyond their existing product line of photocopying. They couldn't figure out how a product which is not related to their main business line, could still have a lot of potential of becoming huge. Many times, our innovations and ideas don't match with our current businesses but that doesn't mean that we should let go of them. Sometimes we have to imagine the future and see if our innovation is making that future better or not. [19]

- No Data Analysis

In digital times, there is an abundance of data like we have never seen before. Now you know more than the age, ethnicity and location of your customers. You know exactly what kind of interests your customers have, what they do in their past time, what other things they shop for, and what kind of political beliefs they have, the list is endless.

Data analysis is like the CCTV footage of your store. You know everything.

The data we collect non-stop from social media, emails, newsletters, Google, Amazon, and other channels is giving us access to a goldmine. When we will finish mining this data, we will realize how it can positively impact our businesses.

Unfortunately, so many of us are still not unlocking the full potential of our data. If only we start doing that, we will see if we are still heading to our desired destination of business growth or we may have derailed a long time ago and are now just going to a place of disappointment and failure.

As a matter of fact, data analysis can answer all of your questions related to how your audience is reacting to your products. That knowledge can help you introduce changes in your products at the right time before your audience gets frustrated for being ignored and decides to switch to your competitors.

Data can also show what the next big thing is going to be. This is how Jeff Bezos came up with the idea of Amazon. Data showed him that online shopping is going to be a big thing and look where he is now. Doesn't it make you want to start reading your data right now?

- Inability to See Trends

On being asked about how he came up with the idea of Amazon, Jeff Bezos said "The wake-up call was finding this startling statistic that web usage in the spring of 1994 was growing at 2,300 percent a year. You know, things just don't grow that fast. It's highly unusual, and that made me think, what kind of business plan might make sense in the context of that growth?" [20]

Jeff Bezos analyzed the data to uncover a trend. This shows us the importance of figuring out trends in time.

Amazon was an example of a company which is built on right trend identification. Now let's discuss another example where a company failed because it didn't recognize a trend on time. This company is Blockbuster. To give you an idea of how big this company was at one point in time, let me share some data about them. Blockbuster once employed over 84,000 people in 9,094 outlets all over the world before Netflix came into existence and started their downfall. In short, their inability to change their business model on time led to their fall.[21]

When it comes to riding a trend for business growth, there are three important steps that we should always remember: data analysis, trend identification and fast and effective decision making.

Only when all the three steps are implemented, we are able to lead our businesses to success.

- Inability to Make Decisions on Time

Market research, data analysis, trend identification - everything becomes useless if the decisions are not made on time. Time plays a very important role in the growth of a business because if your competitor makes an important decision before you do, they will end up becoming the market leader like we have seen in the case of the Xerox computer and the Apple computer. Xerox kept thinking what to do with its computer while Apple wooed the market without any loss of time.

Here's another company which lost its market share because of its inability to make decisions on time. Blackberry once had a loyal customer base of 80 million users, but all those users are now happily using their iPhones.[22] What drove them out of the business was lack of timely and effective decision making! They had failed to implement touchscreen technology in their phones which finally became the strength of Apple's iPhones.

- Unwillingness to Change

The first step of change starts with the willingness to

change. Many times, we are not able to see what this change will bring us in the future or where it will lead us but **ignoring change is a far more risk than following the change**. I still see many people who don't want to change the way they have been doing business. They still think that if they're able to run a successful business for so long without changing, they can continue to do the same.

Most of the initial resistance comes from the inability to overcome this resistance that a new change brings in our lives. We know if we are trying to make our inventory digital, it might need a few days of training everyone which seems like a loss of time. These days you are going to spend just learning and not actually doing something which can show instant results is very scary. But these are the days which actually add a lot of convenience and efficiency in your way of doing the same thing once you get used to it. Not to mention, the efficiency gives you a competitive edge.

- Missing Out on Opportunities

If you want to go big in the business world, you need to have the right product at the right time. If you are trying to market an old TV with a hunch back in 2020, even this book won't work for you. However, if this hunchback TV contains a woofer, a dishwasher, a washer, a dryer and a security AI bot that will catch the intruder and hold them in its arms till the cops arrive, it's your decade. I got carried away a little, phew!

To get back to my point, you can't sell those outdated products of the past right now, especially if they are technology related products. Nobody wants those highly inconvenient and giant phones. Most people do not need those computers with so many attached devices like a CPU, keyboard, mouse and multiple wires. We all have moved to a better version of the same product.

You need to market the right product at the right time. In short, always remember if people have tasted the convenience, ease and time-saving effects of a product, they won't go back. Now, you can't popularize those old cars when we have better, energy-efficient, environment-loving cars. Nobody wants to take a horse cart ride to their destination when they know they can easily fly and reach most of the places in a few hours.

Are You Scared of Taking Risks?

The Story of "What if?"

"What if?" stories are the most painful and hurtful stories for any business owner.
Regret of losing an opportunity to become a highly successful company is unforgettable and you don't want to be a protagonist of any such stories. When you see your competitors rise and leave you behind because they did what you were always scared to, it hurts your business spirit.

Not only will you will not be able to forget about this missed opportunity but even the people around you will never let you forget that. Your business will be talked about in case studies and books and you will be reliving your one mistake over and over again.

The "What if" story of Kodak

Kodak was once the leader in the market of photographic films. One would expect that they should be the ones to know more about the coming shift in customer needs. Maybe they did! What they lost at that time were not insights but courage to take the game-changing risk. They had failed to see that whenever the right risk is taken, the loss was minimal, but profits were high.

When the digital revolution came, Kodak was not ready to take the risk and they couldn't see how this was going to affect the future. Shockingly, they were the first ones to invent the first digital camera, but they thought it would lead to cannibalization of their own products. [23]

So, they didn't tell others about it and kept it a secret. Unluckily, you can't hide trends and innovation. If you won't, someone else will.

The same thing happened even in this case. They didn't launch a digital camera but someone else did. Now, not just their old products were cannibalized as they were fearing but they had even lost the opportunity to gain market share for a product which they'd first invented.

In many countries, they diverted their focus to selling photo albums after having lost the battle of camera and photographic films. What if they hadn't kept their invention of the first digital camera a secret? What if they had slowly let their photographic films die and invested all the resources from that into digital cameras? What if they were still the market leader? I am sure there are so many "what ifs" that must be still troubling them but it's too late now. The opportunity was missed, and the new future has been created by somebody else!

The "What if" story of Xerox

Xerox had a similar story to Kodak. They were the first ones to invent the PC, but the decision makers thought that going digital was very expensive. They had failed to see that there will be a time when people will actually lose interest in paper and pen, and they will start relying on digital technology for all their writing related needs.

Xerox thought it was too risky as technology could fail and this trend would not catch on. Unfortunately, this trend became huge. People have not just moved to digital documents, but they are also loving it. Just imagine what their story would have been today if they would have decided to go digital.

This is something that you don't want to do, you don't want a marketer to write your case in her book like, *17 Reasons Why Businesses Fail.*

The "What if" story of Apple

Let's talk about Apple and how they ride trends without fearing anything. We all are aware of iPods. They became widely successful. Apple took the biggest risk that any business owner fears the most. They'd launched a product which would cannibalize their very much popular iPods. They did this at the time when iPods were recording the highest sales. The product they had launched was the iPhone.

Their head of marketing in an interview when asked on the chances of cannibalization said that "It's not a danger. It's almost by design." Apple not only competes with other products, but they also compete with their own products and that's how they remain a market leader.

So, iPods were cannibalized but the change was necessary as iPhones brought a digital revolution in mobile technology. [24]

Now, imagine what if Apple hadn't launched iPhones? What if somebody else did? Fortunately, Apple's 'what if' story has a happy ending unlike Kodak and Xerox's stories.

Innovation and Opportunity Lies on the Other Side of Risk-Taking

Innovation means you change the way people are seeing or doing something for quite a long time. Expecting people to cast off their old ways of doing an activity and adopting a new one is no doubt very daunting, challenging and frightening but when has change ever been easy?

Change is neither instant nor spontaneous. It's gradual but it's necessary.

Imagine if we still continued using horses instead of cars, seems strange, right? You won't be able to reach wherever you want to go so fast and as easily as you can now. Globalization would have never happened. You wouldn't have explored the wonderful world outside of your own neighborhood.

Henry Ford must have been scared as well when he thought of bringing such a big change into everyone's life. But he still did it because he knew changes can be tough but, in the end we all want something better and something more convenient. For example, I love notebooks, but I still use digital docs. They are faster, better, safer and easily accessible.

The Story of Tom

The concept of Toms is you buy one pair of shoes and they donate one pair of shoes to the ones in need. Doesn't seem like a profitable concept, right? That's what everyone else thought as well. A few people even called this idea insane but the founder, Blake Mycoskie, believed that by passing profits to people in need, he will be able to one day increase his sales which will eventually lead to positive cash flow.

What Blake predicted came true. The company became successful as the concept made people feel good that they are able to help others. Conclusion, TOMS is a multimillion-dollar company now.

No Better Way to Gain Competitive Advantage

The moment you decide to start a business, you are taking a risk of launching something that you don't know is going to succeed or not. Even if it becomes successful, it doesn't mean that your risk-taking journey is over.

If you don't take more risks with time, your business will become stagnant and can start its downfall.

The lifecycle of a highly successful product is like the curve of a hill. It goes down, up and then down again. You experience loss first and then you experience profits which is generally the case with most businesses.

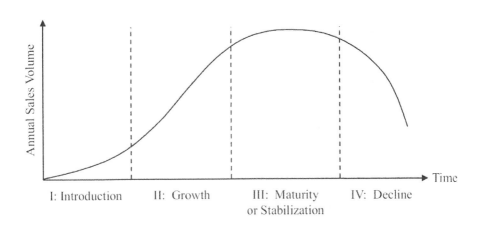

As you can see in the graph, once your product hits the peak of the growth, it starts declining after that. If you want your product to hit another peak, you have to innovate and gain a competitive edge again. Otherwise big market players or other competitors will drive you out of the market.

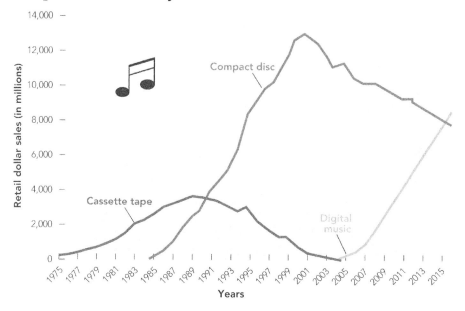

This is a graph of how technological innovations affected the music industry. Every product will hit its peak, and after that, to remain competitive it needs innovation. As you can see in the music industry, the cassette tape led to compact discs, which in turn led to digital music.

The moment you will stop innovating, somebody else will make your product outdated and will become the market leader.

Add 'Calculated' in Your Risk-Taking

You need to be a risk taker, but you have to also make sure that you are a calculated risk taker. You have to see if there is potential in that risk or not; if the trend you are seeing is just a fad. Long-term company growth comes when you're able to make your company disruption-proof.

Taking risks brings success but only if the risk you are taking is the right one. I have seen people who turned many normal day-to-day activities into an inconvenient, more time consuming and complex form with their innovation. Innovations are supposed to make lives easier and not more complicated. A calculated risk-taker will know if the trend you're seeing or expecting is going to add convenience to your customers' lives or not. If the answer is no, it's not going to succeed. If you still take risks, you are just wasting your time waiting for something unexpected to happen.

For example, I can't take the risk to start bringing horses back for transportation now. That time is gone. People have adjusted to the fast speed of cars and convenience that it has brought with it.

The last thing that you should keep in mind is to determine your risk-taking level. If you have $1,000, you can't take a risk of $100,000. This can hurt you badly. Risks are opportunities but they should be accompanied by the right research and right product.

Avoiding Going Digital

What you like is not the same as what others like. You may hate social media, but others may still like it. You have to make decisions according to others.

Many of us still like human interaction when we buy things in store while many others prefer the online shopping as it adds convenience and saves time. I had known many business owners who were still stuck in their old ways and wanted to go back to the times before there was social media and people only visited stores. But they'd failed to realize that technology is unavoidable and it's not about what they feel, it's about what their customers want.

You don't have to force your choices on your customers. If you still haven't still gone digital, think and interact with your customers and ask them if they would prefer the technical version over the current version of your business and if the answer is yes, it's time for you to change before it's too late.

In short, it's better to jump early than late. You have to always be vigilant and make sure you're ready to get on the bandwagon as a need for any new change arises. Most technologies reach their maturity and then a different version is required. If you are late, you might be riding a trend which is already on the verge of disappearance.

To be successful, you have to embrace the change as change is the only constant thing in the business world.

Change comes from innovation and adaptability. When dealing with changes, you will require a new way of thinking, new skills, new tools and new learnings. But in the end, it will all be worth it.

References

18.https://petapixel.com/2010/08/05/the-worlds-first-digital-camera-by-kodak-and-steve-sasson/
19.https://www.businessinsider.com/xerox-was-actually-first-to-invent-the-pc-they-just-forgot-to-do-anything-with-it-2012-2?IR=T
20.https://www.zdnet.com/pictures/amazon-at-20-highs-and-lows/2/
21.https://www.businessinsider.com/the-rise-and-fall-of-blockbuster-video-streaming-2020-1
22.https://www.theverge.com/2012/2/21/2789676/rim-blackberry-mike-lazaridis-jim-balsillie-lost-empire
23.https://www.hbs.edu/openforum/openforum.hbs.org/goto/challenge/understand-digital-transformation-of-business/the-

tragedy-of-kodak.html

24.https://www.businessinsider.com/apple-on-cannibalization-2015-12

CHAPTER 10

Ineffective Marketing and Advertising Plan

"The only form of marketing that works is ethical marketing as it is built on the most-prized asset of the digital age - customer trust." - Pooja Agnihotri

The Story of a Life in Invisibility

Once there was an entrepreneur, Mr. Peter Smith who was working on a great idea. Very unique and in-tune with customer's needs, I will say. The only problem was that he refused to hire any kind of marketing services. He had always believed that a great product like this will not need marketing. That it will sell by itself.

After a year, we talked again. I asked the same question if he is now thinking of adding some kind of marketing plan to his business project. This time the answer was, "I think I just need the right connections and then, they can help me in promoting this product. I need some investors, or some other kind of strong connections."

Another two years passed after that conversation. We connected again. Again I tried to tell him that a product as great and perfect as it can be can't get discovered on its own. Connections can help a little, maybe they can boost your word of mouth marketing but that won't be enough to sustain a business in the long run.

With that statement, I raised the same question, "Do you think about marketing now?" To which he answered, "I think I need to improve my product a little more." He then spends another year with his team perfecting the product, yet the product remained undiscovered by the masses.

We spoke again and I asked the same thing, "What do you think about it now?"

"I think marketing is for big companies. I am a small company. Maybe when my business grows, I will consider marketing," he responded. It's been almost six years since he's started that company and still no one knows about that product.

Do you know when this conversation happened? 2012.

Are you curious to know where that business is now after eight years of existence?
At the same point from where that business started a long time ago. Nobody knows about it and there are no clients for that business.

There is so much to learn from this conversation. A lot of misconceptions about marketing can be seen here. Unfortunately, these misconceptions are very deadly for a business.

1) Misconception 1: Good products don't need marketing.

No product irrespective of how great it is can sell itself without being discovered with the power of marketing. In addition, many good products have failed from a lack of marketing.

2) Misconception 2: Only word-of-mouth marketing is enough.

Word-of-mouth marketing is great. It can help you enter the market, but it cannot help you stay in the market or achieve rapid long-term growth.

Haven't we all seen at least one grocery store in our neighborhood who mainly acquired customers because of a friendly owner and strong word-of-mouth marketing? In the end, they still remained our neighborhood grocery stores before being thrown out of the market by other big grocery chains.

3) Misconception 3: Perfecting a product will help in selling more.

Perfecting a product which is not selling is a waste of time and energy. First, you need to see if this is something that customers want. If not, what aspect of it don't they like? Stop assuming and wasting your time on things which are not important.

The newer version of the product can be more efficient and interesting than the last one but changing a product doesn't alter the business situation of invisibility and anonymity.

For example, I bake great pot pies. I hope that one day everybody will know how good I am at making those delicious flaky pies. For the same reason, I keep perfecting my pot pies within the four walls of my home, without ever letting the outside world know what they have been missing. After a few years, I have a super delicious pot pie but still I live in anonymity. The moral of the story is: get the word out, don't wait until somebody stumbles upon your product.

4) Misconception 4: Marketing is not just for big companies.

Marketing is for everyone. How do the companies become big? By doing marketing. Their growth doesn't happen overnight. Everyone didn't wake up one day and realize that Coca Cola and Apple are the biggest brands.

To get back to the point, you need way more marketing in the beginning because nobody knows you. Now, you have to introduce yourself to customers, make them familiar with you before you can ask them to buy from you. For that, you will need marketing.

In reality, small companies and start-ups need marketing more than big organizations. The current market is way too competitive and you can't get yourself heard in this crowd without a good marketing strategy.

Marketing is an investment. Don't treat it like sales. Don't think that if you pay $1,000, you're going to see results worth $2,000 in the very beginning especially if you are a new company. You are not selling, you are marketing. Marketing is all about building a brand and increasing your brand equity. People might not buy from you right when you start marketing your product, but they are going to remember you, or they will learn something about you.

Business growth happens when people remember you. The next time they get thirsty, they will remember Coca Cola, the next time they want to go on a vacation with their kids, they will remember Disneyland, when they want to buy an engagement ring, they will remember DeBeers and when they need a product that you sell, they will remember your brand. In short, you do marketing if you want to be remembered later.

Just like the long-term stock market investment, your marketing efforts will also multiply many times.

The Untold Story of Marketing

The biggest secret of your business success lies in marketing.

MARKETING!
This word scares a lot of people because most of them don't know anything about it and as humans, we are fearful of anything unknown. Isn't that the reason why we are scared of alien life, unknown places and surprisingly, even humans who are of different religion, race, nationality or culture than ours?

The fear of the unknown is deadly for our personal growth as well as for the growth of our business.

You will be surprised to know that marketing is present in every stage of our lives. We have been reaping its benefits for so long without even realizing it. The only problem is we just never used the word 'marketing' to describe those particular actions.

Remember the efforts you put in to make your resume appealing and perfect. That's marketing! In a way, it resembles print marketing as we see in flyers and brochures. Now, think of all the hard work that went into sending your kids to that perfect school you've always wanted them to attend. That involved marketing as well. It was a combination of network marketing, branding, and direct advertising. Let's not forget all those dates you have been on. What you did on those dates was an example of branding where you tried to form the right and favorable image of yours in your date's mind.

Marketing works and that's why we use it so often in our day to day lives: consciously and unconsciously. Sometimes it is disguised as we have seen in the examples above but it's always there - helping and shaping our lives for better and positive results.

If our personal lives need marketing, how can we even think that our business can go on without it?

Each and every kind of business is dependent on marketing. It's the basic requirement for the survival and growth of your business.

What Happens When Businesses Don't Market Themselves?

Here are the golden words to guide you:

"A bad product may or may not succeed with marketing, but a good product will definitely never succeed without proper marketing."

Just creating a product isn't enough if you're going to keep that product locked in a box on a deserted island. Maybe after hundreds of years, somebody will discover it accidentally. But after those hundreds of years, you won't be there, your audience won't be the same and even their needs won't be the same. Sadly, your product will be of no use to them after all those years because of it being outdated!

Just imagine what will happen if many of the old products are sold in current times like a giant computer where you have to punch in your instructions and then wait for many hours before the computer is ready to respond.

In present times, more and more women are working, the LGBTQ community has become an important part of our society, many men are now full-time dads, the old philosophy of two kids and two cars has lost its charm and a large percentage of households are now made up of single parents, couples with no kids, and unrelated people living together. All these changes will make it tough for any old product to gain success now.

Humans evolve with time and so do their needs.

Either you can wait to be discovered but you will be taking a risk against the changes that time brings with it. The risk of selling a product to a changing audience, transforming technology, evolving needs, and depleting resources. Or you can speed up the process of your product discovery before any such change leaves your product outdated and unwanted with the help of marketing.

It's simple - as an employee, you can either wait for a good company to discover your potential in a market of so many candidates or you can speed up the entire process with the help of marketing and get a job way faster than you would have got in the first case.

Poor Marketing is Equally as Bad as No Marketing

Many times, stunted business growth happens because of poor marketing. When I say poor marketing, I mean ineffective marketing that doesn't produce the expected results for a business. Sometimes it can even damage your current standing in the market.

There can be various reasons why your marketing is not working:

- Poor Market Research

  I call it one of the biggest mistakes any business owner or entrepreneur can make - the mistake of not knowing well your target market, audience and their needs. Incorrect results of the market research when fed to the marketing strategy and action plans produce disastrous results. When you lay a weak foundation, then you cannot expect an amazing outcome.

- No Marketing Strategy

Yes, a strategy is very important as this is the only thing that will help you in being heard, seen and loved in a crowd of millions and even billions. If your current strategy is to use somebody else's strategy or copy a marketing strategy template you found on the internet, you might be disappointed to see the final result.

The copied strategy won't help you stand apart. This will still keep you hidden in the crowd. In addition, no two businesses have the same market, product, customer needs and consequently, no two businesses can have the same strategy. If you can find another business that has everything the same just like you, then you have to rethink your product and your business idea.

- Missing Data Analysis

The best part about digital marketing and digital advertising is that we have access to data related to our every digital action. If we are not measuring the results of our marketing strategies, then we are just hitting in the dark when we can switch on the lights and efficiently aim at our target. The purpose of data is to learn on time what is working and what is not and take any corrective actions according to that. This will make sure that the errors are not propagated.

- Insufficient Budget

In the end, there is a big trade-off between the time and money that you want to invest in your business. You can either save money or you can save time. You can start with a smaller marketing budget than usual, but that means you have to increase the time when you can expect to see the results.

So, if you were planning to make X amount of sales with a Y marketing budget in two years, then, anything lower than Y budget is not going to bring you X amount of sales in two years. Now, the chances are you will see the result in either four years or more than that, depending on where in your marketing budget you're making those deductions.
You can either achieve results fast with a sufficient marketing budget or you can save the money from your marketing budget and increase the time of achieving those results.

- Wrong Marketing Technique

If your technique is wrong, how can you expect the right results? A marketing technique is wrong if it is not based on proper research, not aligned with your long- term goals, and not in tune with your vision.

One more thing that you have to remember is that marketing is not there to misguide, cheat, or sell a wrong product. Marketing needs to be ethical. Anything which is not is generally a wrong marketing technique. You can force a person to buy a product by hiding some of the information or by not sharing enough information. But this technique is not going to make that customer loyal to you. That's why a right and ethical marketing technique is the only way to grow in the market. Don't hide your products' faults but work on those.

- Focusing on Wrong Marketing Channels

The digital world has opened so many marketing channels for us. Let's just take for an example the number of social media sites available. Additionally, we have YouTube, Podcast, Soundcloud and loads more.

Not all these channels are meant for every business. It all depends on where your target audience spends their most time. For your business, YouTube can be a great channel while for somebody else TikTok can be the key. Viber is very much in use in Asian market, so it can be a good channel for them.

In short, you don't have to focus on every channel unless and until you have lots of resources. Unfortunately, most of the business owners have limited resources, and those resources need to be put to the right use. So, figure out what all channels are going to help you in reaching your goals and start working.

- Overpromising and Underdelivering

Often times business owners just for the sake of attracting customers start overpromising even though it is nearly impossible to deliver those results. What happens because of overpromise and underdeliver, you create dissatisfaction and risk your customer's trust. It's always better to overdeliver rather than to underdeliver.

If you think, you can't design a website in two weeks, be upfront with your client. If you think your product's fabric is not 100% cotton, then don't say that, if you think your product is not going to last for more than two years without breaking down, then don't promote it as something which will last five years.

Alternatively, you can focus on your other strengths. Maybe you'll require more time but your website design is impeccable, maybe the fabric of the dress is not 100% cotton but the softness of the fabric is to die for, maybe your product won't last two years but you are going to get more of your money's worth in those two years of its life and after that your customers can get the parts replaced at a cheaper rate.

- Failure to Communicate Values

The most important task of marketing is to communicate the value of your product to your audience. When you're doing no marketing, you're not doing anything to communicate that value. If people don't know the value, they won't buy it.

In some other cases, you are doing marketing but you're not doing the right marketing. In this way, the value is not communicated as well.

Let's say you are launching a vacuum cleaner which takes 20% less energy and is noise free. Then your target audience needs to know these points. They don't need to know that the product is of good quality. But they need to know exactly how your product is of better quality and what your product benefits are over your competitors.

When a value is communicated well, it gives your potential customers an option to choose you over others and to stick to your brand.

- Targeting Everyone

Here comes the biggest marketing problem which is generally seen in most of the ineffective marketing plans. Most of the business owners feel so tempted to include everyone in their target audience so that they can convert more of those people into their customers. Only 3.1% of all the beverages consumed around the world belong to Coca Cola. If they can't convert everyone as their customers with a big marketing and advertising budget. How do you think you can?

We fail to see that people are very different, their preferences are different and in no possible scenario is everyone going to like our product. There are many people who don't like Apple products, and even Starbucks coffee just because they have different choices. This is the first thing you have to accept before you implement your marketing plan.

Anyhow, your target audience can't be women of New York City. Within that group, there are many subsets already. If you're launching a beauty product, you have to target those women who love the kind of cosmetics that you are selling and are in the right age range. Vegan cosmetic lovers, paraben-free cosmetic lovers, organic cosmetic lovers, luxury cosmetic lovers, or something else; choices of people within the set of cosmetics lovers can vary a lot.

You can always expand later if you think that another set of audience can also consider your product if the message is communicated well. But this can't be done when you are starting a business because in the latter case, you are trying to bring a huge cultural change and changes take a lot of time, energy and money. In the beginning, you have to use your resources wisely.

In sum, marketing is very essential for a business. Even though marketing is one of the building blocks of a successful business, we should make sure that our marketing is effective and productive.

In addition, you have to make decisions about your marketing budget. Do you want to save your money by cutting down your marketing budget at the wrong places and opting for an ineffective form of marketing instead? For example, eliminating brand awareness ad campaigns from your marketing plan because they don't immediately convert your audience to your customers. Such decisions will provide you with short term gratification when you will save a little money from your marketing budget, but it won't build a brand or bring long-term growth for you.

Understanding the Process of Advertising

Advertising plays an important role in increasing your reach to your potential customers and making people aware of your product. Each and every type of business will need customers to survive and grow. For getting those customers, you need to first let them know about your business, your product and how your product is exactly what they are looking for. And for that very purpose, you have to advertise your product.

Failing to understand the importance of advertising can drive your business to failure. In one of my conversations with an entrepreneur, I was told that she doesn't do brand awareness ad campaigns as it is just a waste of her ad budget and she only wants ads that bring instant sales. Like many others, she's also failed to realize that brand awareness is the way to sales. Your business can't directly jump from being an unknown product to a high-selling product business.

The Process of Advertising

Advertising converts strangers into customers through a four-step process:

- First, it generates awareness about your product.
- Once people become aware of your product, it makes them develop an interest in your product, so they consider buying it.
- Once they consider buying it, advertising lets them compare your product with other competing products in the market.
- When the comparison phase is over, advertising lets your audience buy your product.

Why Advertising is Needed

for Business Growth

Advertising is very powerful as it brings a business out of the darkness to the light and brings your products closer to your buyers. You can only sell a product if people know that you exist. If your target audience doesn't even know that there is a product out there which can fill the gap created by their needs, why would they ever consider buying from you?

Here's why you need advertising.

Advertising
- Improves your brand awareness and brings new customers.
- Generates brand loyalty and leads to repeat customers.
- Helps your business compete with others which leads to competitors' customers switching to your product.
- Improves your business image.
- Increases web and foot traffic.
- Makes sure that your customers never forget you.
- Builds brands.
- Adds credibility to your business.
- Helps to communicate with your customers.
- Makes your customers continue using your products and not switch to other options.
- Helps in bringing back all those customers who switched to other options.

The Gap Between Advertising and Effective Advertising

There is a difference between advertising and effective advertising. If you want your business to succeed, you need effective advertising. Which means showing the right ad at the right time to the right people in the right context, so they take action. If any of those things (time, target audience, place, or context) is not right, the ad won't produce the desired results.

Ineffective advertising leads to loss of your ad budget and can even hurt your brand image. An effective ad brings long-term positive residual effects for your business. A good ad, and its influence isn't easily forgotten. It builds a brand, creates a bond with your customers and makes them nostalgic every time they see your ad.

Short-term Versus Long-term Benefits of Advertising

Many times, you won't see the effects from an ad campaign instantly but that should not discourage you from investing in advertising as this is one of the reasons how Coca Cola built such a huge brand. Sometimes when you invest $1,000, you don't get $2,000 right away in return, sometimes you get $100,000 in a few years.
Advertising is like a stock market for your business investment.

All you need to do is be patient. If a set of people who have seen your ad and still haven't bought anything from you, then you can confuse that ad as an ineffective ad. But it's not. If the same set of people still remember you ten years after that ad was run and tell people about you, then this is a success. As I've stated previously, when people remember you, growth happens.

As a result, it becomes very important to not lose patience and focus more on the long-term benefits of an ad rather than the immediate ones.

When is an Ad Campaign Considered Ineffective?

There are still so many people out there who give the task of handling their social media channels to their family members or the task of SEO to some inexperienced professional just to cut down the costs. Let me give you a little idea of how these kinds of cost-cutting can affect your long-term growth.

First, we have to understand that the digital world is just like the real world. In the real physical world, you won't ask your family member to prepare a billboard or TV ad for you because you don't want to mess with the reputation of your brand that you have built over many years. You don't want people to misinterpret your message. You practice extreme caution.

But you forget that social media is made from the same people who you were targeting with your perfectly designed billboard advertising. On the other hand, now your brand will be exposed to a bigger audience than a billboard would have made it. When your audience hasn't changed and the size of your audience has gone up, how come you are comfortable playing with your brand image with those poorly formed social media posts and ads? In the end, the cost of fixing your damaged brand image can prove way more expensive and time-consuming.

There are various reasons why an ad doesn't work as it should. Here's when your ad becomes ineffective:

1. Your ad is ignored by the masses and the message is lost.

   This is the main problem of online advertising. Majority of the online ads are ignored. Interestingly, it seems like the present time people have evolved to ignore online ads. Just like selective listening, now we have selective ad viewing. That's how the banner blindness came into being.

2. Your ad is too boring that it is not able to gain or retain attention.

Digital trends have made it easy to run ads for each and every business type irrespective of the business size. The ease of advertising on social media and on other digital channels make it seem like that they don't deserve as much attention as TV ads, but this is what leads to the creation of extremely boring ads. And being boring is what makes your audience ignore you.

3. Your message is so confusing that viewers don't know what you are trying to communicate.

Many times, when an ad gets over, viewers aren't able to figure out the purpose of that ad, the kind of product that was advertised, why was that product worth consideration or what actually the brand wants them to do. If you want to have an effective ad, you need to work on communicating your message in the most effective way. Keep it clear, concise and non-confusing.

4. Your ad doesn't have the right strategy or goals.

In business, everything is based on strategy from recruitment to advertising. An advertising strategy is based on proper research which guides you in this entire process of customer acquisition with the help of ads.

5. Your ad is not targeted to the right audience, making it totally irrelevant.

Have you ever seen an ad which is something that you will never need or is irrelevant to your current life stage? Such ads only make your audience frustrated.

6. Your ad spend is not enough to generate the expected outcome.

In a case like this, everything is right about the ad except the budget. Sometimes the budget cuts are made in advertising which hurts the purpose of running an ad. For example, you can't expect to build a big brand with just $10,000 worth of advertising. If it was possible, everyone would have taken a loan, borrowed some money and became the Starbucks of their market.

One of the business owners I knew kept reducing the advertising budget month after month until it became negligible just because he was not able to see the results instantly. Long story short, that product is dead now.

7. Your ad is good but your presence on other channels is not.

For example, your potential customer sees your ad, then decides to check out your social media page but your social media doesn't show an appealing picture. Maybe you're not active there, maybe nobody engages with you there or maybe you have posted something there which goes against your customer's values. As a result, it will ultimately lead your customer to change their mind.

8. When your ads lack creative vision.

This is what gives life to your ad. Creativity is something which can make your ads highly memorable which will make it easier for your potential customers to remember you.

When the time comes for the advertising, remember to make it effective, memorable and innovative. After all, a good ad is worth so much more than just a little ad spend. A bad ad costs way more than your investment. It hurts your bond with your customers, builds false expectations and creates wrong perceptions.

CHAPTER 11

Unbalanced Three Pillars of Marketing

"You are dealing with emotional customers and not analytical bots." - Pooja Agnihotri

The Story of Too Much Data

This is not a story of one company, but almost of 90% of the companies these days. Back when I'd first started my marketing career and looking for job opportunities with a marketing company, wherever I applied and wherever I went for the interview, they all had one thing in common - data-driven marketing. Data-driven means that they focus on data, they analyze data, and they form their strategies based on data.

The term data-driven always made me wonder about creativity. How many numbers do we remember? How many creative ideas in the form of ads, music, movies, books, and other forms of arts do you remember? I am sure the answer for the latter will be higher than the first one. If creativity was not so important, Manhattan Avenue creative directors and copywriters wouldn't be paid so much and hired by all the big ad agencies.

Earlier the creativity was mainly meant for the ad agencies. That's why they were called creative agencies. If you want an ad you go to a creative agency. But the advent of digital advertising has started blurring this line between a marketing agency and an ad agency.

As digital advertising has become more affordable for all, many business owners have started approaching digital marketing companies to run their ads rather than approaching ad agencies who mainly work on multimillion-dollar ad campaigns. If a marketing agency is going to create ads, it can't rely on just data as its strength but will also rely on creativity like traditional ad agencies.

When I'd became a part of Bizadmark and started interacting with clients, I've realized that even they have been enamored by the word data-driven and creativity has kind of taken a back seat.

There are many things that numbers don't show us right away. There are many things your Google analytics and social media analytics will not tell you in a month and even in a year's time like familiarity with your brand, bonding with your brand, the feeling of nostalgia, memorability and many things like that. For all those invisible and uncountable benefits, you focus on creativity.

Three Pillars

The reason that online ads are 80% of the time ignored lies in the fact that we have started forgetting creativity when creativity is as important as data.[25]

Before you work on your marketing plan, you need to know that there are three important pillars on which the success of your marketing campaign as well as your business growth is going to depend. These are strategic, analytic and creative pillars. Now, you have to learn to use the three in a complete balance, so your business can grow.

Strategic Pillar

Before digital times, we were actively advertising on various non-digital channels like magazines, TV, radio, billboard, direct mails and trade shows. Interestingly, whenever any decision was taken to advertise at any of these channels, it was followed by a lot of research and planning. A company wouldn't just decide in the morning that we wanted a billboard ad on that highway and by the evening, it would be there. Everything followed a process before an ad was finalized and made public.

For example, a TV ad involves at least four months of research and creative brainstorming. How much planning and research do we add in our digital advertising campaigns now? A few hours! Maybe a few days! Then, we wonder why our ads are not making an impact and are ignored all the time.

When I had worked as a marketer for a company, the CEO asked me to run Facebook, Instagram, Google and Bing ads in just four hours. He didn't understand the importance of marketing based on a strategy. And that's the kind of mistake many business owners are still making - failing to see the side effects of bad marketing and advertising campaigns.

A good marketing plan can't be formed in just four hours. Plans are formed on extensive research. As in the case above, the CEO was targeting four channels - Facebook, Instagram, Google and Bing.

All these channels are used for different purposes and have different kinds of audiences. Without researching about these differences in relation to a product and understanding how to use those strategically to advertise an ad, you'll end up throwing your money away.

Many of my clients still ask me how I'm going to market their product and they expect that my answer will be that we'll use social media, email, content, google ads, SEO, radio ads, etc. or a combination of some of them. The answer is not what kind of digital channels I'm going to use, but what kind of strategy I'm going to use. If the strategy requires us to use social media, we will use social media. If the strategy requires us to focus mainly on Facebook and not on any other social media, we will do that.

A strategy is an action plan of what you want to achieve and how. It defines where you want to see yourself in the long-term and how you are going to use your resources, skills and competencies to achieve that.

There are no strategies available on the internet that you can copy and use for your own business. These are generally created based on your business model, your product, your point of differentiation from others, your available resources, business goals, business environment and a lot more. These factors are not the same for everyone and as a result, every business requires a unique strategy.

Strategies can't be created in a day. So, if your question is, what kind of strategy are you going to use for my business? I won't be able to instantly answer you because strategies require research which requires time.

Why is Strategy Important?

Strategy is like an action plan to reach your goals. Without this, you are just hitting in the dark and hoping that you will hit the target. I won't say that it can't happen but 99.9% of the time it will fail. You can waste your resources and hope that you fall in the category of 0.1% or you can ditch that category and join the one where the probability of hitting your goals is much higher.

Strategy makes sure that all your resources are used efficiently, that your efforts will convert into the desired outcome and that you are heading in the direction of your goal. Without a strategy, you will confuse merely posting on social media channels as marketing. When you use a strategy, your social media channels show the results you want to see as they are advancing in the direction of your business goals. Without a strategy, your social media channels just become a source of entertainment rather than lead-generation tools.

Tips for Creating an Effective Strategy

1. Don't Use Digital Channels Without Strategy

If you use any digital channel like social media, website, search engine or emails without any strategy, the results might not be as per your expectation. You will lose your time and money running ineffective social media campaigns, email marketing campaigns or something else.

In the end, you will be left with two options - to quit that campaign or to start from the scratch. Making a mistake like this is quite draining and unmotivating. That's why it's better to start right the very first time.

2. Don't Copy Somebody Else's Strategy

Copying somebody else's strategy is something you want to avoid at all costs.

This is true that there are so many templates available on the internet. All you have to do is type marketing strategy for restaurant, social media strategy for ecommerce, and you will get a plethora of results.

However, these templates can't still be used as these results are generic. You can get an idea based on these to create your own but you can't use them to completely replace your own unique strategy. An online restaurant marketing template will still not tell you how the market of New York is totally different from the market of Louisville and how your marketing campaign is actually dependent on these differences.

Your business is unique, and so are your business goals. In case you think you should be allowed to copy somebody else's strategy because you think the business in the template matches yours, then you're in even deeper trouble. Furthermore, you should get branding services straightaway to make yourself unique. No business has become big because it was just like others. We don't have a second Amazon or a second McDonald's.

A product which is undifferentiated is bound to fail. If your product is differentiated, then there won't be any strategy available online for you.

You can borrow somebody else's dress for a party, but you might have to use a lot of alterations, safety pins and in the end, it is still not going to be the same as a dress perfectly tailored to your size.

3. Don't Forget to Monitor the Performance of Your Strategy

A strategy is not permanent. It's like water, it will keep changing itself as the obstacles come.

Sticking to one strategic plan is not the road to success. You have to keep your strategy easily adaptable according to the changing situation. When you implement a strategy, many unexpected situations come.

The business environment changes. The technology evolves. As a result, we adapt and change our strategy to take into consideration any unexpected scenarios that may have arisen.

Creative Pillar

Everything needs to be done strategically as well as creatively. The race to get more and more data has taken our focus off the creativity. But creativity is not some kind of fad. It is still as important as it has always been.

When technology takes over every aspect of our lives, we won't care anymore about the data but poems, songs, paintings and other creative arts.

To get back to the point, you must have encountered a lot of data in your life, how much do you remember now? Now think about all the stories you have heard, how many of them do you remember? Which one made a better impact on you? Numbers or stories? The answer is definitely going to be stories, unless you are a bot reading this.

Stories are emotional and powerful, and they connect us to our humanness.

Numbers are emotionless and very analytical in nature, but humans are not analytical, they are emotional.

Have you ever had employees who took half the day off because they were having family issues, employees who were distracted at the office because they had just been engaged, employees who were not working to their fullest because they were overpowered by some kind of emotion? You must have!

This happens because **when it comes to humans, things are not as simple as black and white. There is a whole range of gray**

shades between the two.

That is why, if your audience is made up of humans, you need to add the element of creativity in addition to data. But if your audience is bots, then you're good to go unless the robots are from the show "Raised by Wolves."

Why Is Creativity Important?

If we look at the data, we will learn these few things:

- Online advertising has brought the cost of advertising down. Now, people who have millions of dollars for their ad campaigns are not the only ones capable of advertising.

   Most of the new business owners can't advertise on TV or radio but they can easily do video advertising on YouTube and Facebook, and Radio lookalike advertising on Podcasts.

- As the barrier to advertise has gone down, more and more businesses have started advertising. That means that now consumers will be shown way more ads than they were in the past. Surrounded by so many ads, they will remember only a few creative ones.

   As the ads are now being served to consumers 24X7 and not just through the radio or TV, the consumers are growing less tolerant to irrelevant and boring ads. In addition, online advertising is becoming the most ignored form of advertising. Do you remember any cool ad that you saw recently? Do you remember any ads before the internet took over? I am sure many because the advertising was a way more creative and well-researched process back then.

   This tells us that the ability to gain and retain attention will be prized even more now. The question now comes whether you want to be among the 80% of the ignored ads or 20% of the well-received ads. If you are choosing the latter, then you can't achieve that without any form of creativity in your ads. As creativity is responsible for making your ads more memorable, catchy and make people nostalgic even after many years from now.

What Happens When You're Not Creative?

Many unwanted things happen when we stop being creative, here are some of them:

- Getting Comfortable with Boring

  You read it right! You get comfortable with being boring which is very deadly for you and your business because nobody likes boring things. In the digital world where we have everything in excess - more social media channels than we can follow, more ads than our brains can process, more emails than we can open, more blogs than we can read; another addition of a boring social media account, newsletter or blog won't gain the attention of your customers.

- Accepting Being Ignored as Normal

  When our ads are ignored, our emails are not opened, our blogs are not read, our videos are not watched or our podcasts are not listened to, we start accepting the results as being normal.

  We think it has happened because the world has changed, people have changed, there are too many ads out there, people are not reading emails anymore or only a few lucky ones hit the jackpot and you're too late in this race. We keep making excuses so as to make ourselves accept being ignored as something normal. But it's not!

You need to break through this noise, be heard, seen and loved. You have to keep trying and stop accepting no for an answer.

The path to success is paved with the bricks of creativity. So, if you think you don't want to be ignored, think how you're going to stand apart from this crowd.

- Focusing on Numbers and Forgetting Stories
Why do humans always tell stories? Why do we teach young kids various important life lessons with the help of stories? As stories create the impact that we want to create. We can tell people either that this many people had lost their lives in World War 2 or we can share stories in the form of movies like Pianist and The Schindler's List. The latter will remain in our memories for way longer.

This is the reason why we remember the movies but hardly remember any presentations or meetings we attend because movies tell stories and presentations share numbers. So, start adding more stories into your brand. It will make you more unique and creative.

Analytic Pillar

I know I focus a lot on creativity but that doesn't mean that I am against numbers. I have always loved mathematics, a subject which I've always excelled in. I had also scored the highest on the global mathematical talent probe during my student days.

I don't mean to brag but it's just a trait of being an Asian. (Just kidding!)

To resume, I love numbers just as much as I love creativity. But the two things need to be in perfect harmony. We need to use numbers to direct our creativity efforts and use creativity to give life to our boring numbers.

Why Are Analytics Important?

Unlike olden times, now we have access to data for everything. We know what our audience is looking for, what they are searching, what they are buying, how much time they spend on various websites, what kind of interests they have and much more. That's why paying attention to your data becomes important.

If youngsters between the ages of 20-30 don't fall in your target audience, then running even the most creative ads will not get you results. This is where numbers play an important role. You read them to figure out who is showing interest in your product and who is not. You can even learn who to target and why, what kind of product features they are going to love and what changes you can make so your product becomes more desirable to them. Then, you can use that data to refine your strategy and give the right direction to all your campaigns.

What Happens When You Don't Listen to Data?

- You Paint a False Picture

  Without data, getting lost is nothing but obvious. Data is what tells you where you are and where you can be. It's like the coordinates for your destination. If you don't have the coordinates, you are just walking on a random path hoping that it will take you to your destination.

  I have seen many people who have completely wrong information about their own businesses. For example, confidently thinking that their target audience are women in the age group of 20-40 years, but data says otherwise.

- Budget Is Misused

  If you don't have the right data, you will spend a lot of your marketing budget on ineffective strategies. For example, you might end up spending a lot on advertising when the actual problem would not be related to brand awareness but to an unfriendly checkout process.

  In a case like that, data can easily show you where the problem is and how to fix it. You can read your website data and see how many people are exiting from the checkout page of your website. Based on that, you can spend your marketing budget in making the checkout process smoother for your web visitors rather than increasing the budget of your brand awareness campaigns. Data puts a stamp on your assumptions when they are right.

- Goals Become Tougher to Achieve

  Let's look at this way. If you are going to LA from NYC and after every half an hour, you can check where you are on the map, then you will know if you are heading in the right direction or not. If you're not heading in the right direction, you will have enough time to change your path and head in the direction of your destination.

  If you don't check, you won't be able to correct the wrong direction you're heading toward and instead continue going further and further in the opposite direction of your destination to LA.

Numbers work the same way. If you check the numbers after a few months and see where your business has reached, you will have enough time to make amends in your strategy. This way you will never lose the focus of your goals and will reach your destination much faster.

Remember, data is not just the street signs, it is the GPS.

- Strategies Fail

Strategies are based on research and data. If you feed the right numbers, your strategy becomes more powerful than ever. If you feed assumptions, misconceptions, guesses and wrong data to your strategy, your strategy becomes worthless but also detrimental to your survival.

If you feel like your strategies are not performing well, then you need to refine it with the help of some good, old, helpful data.

Data is the main reason why your strategy can never be permanent because as you collect more data, you'll use that data to redefine your strategy and this is a never-ending process.

- You Miss Trends and Threats

This is the most important reason why you should start listening to your numbers. Forget about survival and growth for some time. Numbers can give you exponential, once-in-a-lifetime, you-were-lucky kind of a growth.

When you are playing with numbers, you can see many things that others have not yet noticed. You can learn the change in behavior of your customers, change in their needs, or something different which is rising very fast. Then, you can capitalize on that.

There was a time when the use of the internet was skyrocketing and that's when Jeff Bezos decided to start Amazon. He'd read the numbers and caught the trend. You can do that too, if you start understanding the importance of numbers.

Balancing These Three Pillars for Business Growth

These three pillars define your business growth because you need all three if you want to grow. Having just one is not enough. Let's say you are a highly creative company, but you lack strategy and analytics which hinders your growth. If it was not the case, all the artists would have been doing really amazing.

Same with analytics, just having numbers can't do anything for you. As I've explained, humans don't remember numbers, but numbers are good in guiding us where to go.

Strategy is your war plan. If you go to a war without your strategy, you might not be able to defeat the enemy. But if you work on a winning war strategy first, try to anticipate all the enemy moves, devise your actions according to that and train your team to be able to handle various scenarios, you will definitely emerge victorious.

With proper strategy, if you enter a war, you can defeat even the biggest army otherwise you can be defeated by even the smallest army.

Let's take for example The Battle of Marathon from 490 BCE. A battle when the Persian ships entered Greece. The Greek army was not prepared for this. Outnumbered two-to-one, Greeks opted for a brave strategy. They'd kept the Persian army pinned down at Marathon, blocking both the exits and avoiding the possibility of being defeated. The Greeks won the battle.[26]

Maintaining a healthy balance of analytics, strategy and creativity is very important as they're all equally important. The first thing you have to ensure if you plan to be in the business for long is not letting one pillar overpower the other. Take support of these three pillars and watch yourself succeed.

References

25.https://www.businesswire.com/news/home/20140211005607/en/Goo-Study-Ignore-Online-Ads
26.https://historycollection.com/david-beat-goliath-10-small-armies-defeated-large-ones/

CHAPTER 12

Unpreparedness to Fight Off Competition

"Play to win, not 'not to lose." — Dondi Scumaci

The Story of Overconfidence

A long time ago, I was talking to my friend, Victor Davis, who had just started working on his start-up. Here is how the conversation went between the two of us:

Pooja: Who are your competitors?
Victor: No one. There is no such product in the market. It's a billion-dollar idea.
Pooja: There is always competition. There is no such perfect product in the world that exists without any competition. If you still think that you don't have any competitors, try to think about some indirect ones.
For example, Coca Cola doesn't just face competition from other soft drinks but also from water or any other drink that can be used to quench one's thirst. People can always choose water over Coca Cola, thus making water an indirect competitor for them. So, who do you think are your indirect competitors?

Victor: No one! I am telling you it's a unique product.

This conversation happened almost eight years ago, and that start-up is still struggling in the market.

In all honesty, this has been the thought process of many entrepreneurs. Eight out of ten are going to say something similar and this is going to become a reason for their failure in the future. As a result, it becomes a must for every business owner to pay attention to these mistakes that others have made and avoid repeating them.

The two important things that can be taken away from this conversation are:

1. Don't Underestimate Others

It's good to believe in your idea but don't become too cocky with that. Always remember that only when we accept that there is always someone who can do what we are doing, we will learn to evolve. In addition, we get creative and think of various ways of improving our product and filling the gaps created by customer needs better than others.

For the growth of a business, we have to evolve whenever the time, environment and people around us change. For the same reason, you can't feel satisfied that you have designed a perfect product. In the field of business, such thoughts prove very detrimental.

2. If You Exist, So Do Your Competitors

If you think your products are infallible, you will never figure out ways to make them better. This will provide a big advantage to your competitors. When you rejoice for having created the best product in the market, they will work non-stop to figure out how to make what you made - just better.

Don't forget that there is always competition. It can be direct, or it can be indirect, and you should always be prepared with a plan to fight it.

With that being the case, you can't escape the competition. That's why you have to learn how to fight it and win the battle. If your product doesn't have any competition now, it will soon. Lyft, an on-demand ridesharing service, comes into the market, so do Uber and Via. Similarly, Facebook enters the market, and soon various other social media sites come into existence as well. If those big ideas can have competition, so can your idea.

Inability to Survive Competition

The main reason why many business owners fail to survive competition in their industry is because of their attitude and self-assurance. No one is invincible in the business world.

Many business owners find their product so flawless that they ignore any possibility of another similar product or a similar or better substitute. The moment we fail to accept that competition can exist even for the most divine product on this earth, we fail to plan for survival and survive the competition.

Even if you can make a good product, there will always be someone who can show your customers why their product is better than yours or a better alternative than your product.

Once you accept that competition is unavoidable, you can then work on a strategy on how you are going to deal with it. Prepare a detailed plan outlining the current environment in your industry, how easy it is to enter the market, what your strengths are to capitalize on and what weaknesses you need to work on.

The Rise of Photographers

Photography used to be a very exclusive industry where only those who had the experience, expertise, and the ability to buy expensive cameras were able to enter the field.

Not everybody could have been a photographer. People needed to learn how to use those cameras, the perfect angles, in addition gain experience mastering those actions for quite some time.

Then, came the flood of electronic cameras in the market. Nikon and Canon started releasing camera after camera. With each one being better than the previous one. And with that the bar to enter this industry became extremely low.

All those photography businesses who were prepared to fight it off survived this flood, but all those who've never thought that there can be competition or too much competition, eventually your customer is going to be deluged with so many alternatives to the point you're wiped off the market.

Not just that, then came mobile phones with expert cameras and now the customers were burdened with another choice of whether to pick a substitute or the original product. Many customers did pick the substitute of getting pictures taken on their own phones rather than getting a shoot done. Who knew that a substitute can be as powerful as the main product? The moral of the story is to never underestimate your substitute products. They can replace you if you take them lightly.

Tips for Surviving Competition Better Than Most

- Prepare Early

If you want to emerge as a market leader in your industry, you should start preparing early. The sooner you decide to start, the bigger advantage you will gain over your competitors. If you don't start on time but others do, then they will get a head start. This can make it tough for you to survive in the market.

Let's try to understand this with the help of an example. Let's imagine that your presence on the internet is weak and you are not easily searchable by your customers on Google. So, you contact a few digital marketing companies but ultimately decide to hire none. Maybe because you don't have enough budget or maybe because you thought this is not so urgent at the moment. So, to save money, you end up giving the task of SEO (improving your presence on search engines) to your neighbor's daughter who seems to understand a little about it. She doesn't have much experience, but she can do it for real cheap. So, you decide to save some money and go ahead with assigning the work to her.

But your competitor, on the other hand, hires a professional SEO agency from New York. An agency that understands how algorithms work and what kind of approach and strategy can lead to improving the visibility of a business.

In the beginning, as SEO is a slow process, you won't notice any results for your business as well as your competitors' results. This will give you a little relief that you have made the right decision by not hiring an expensive marketing agency.

However, after a few months, you will see that your competitor is now on the sixth page of Google, who was earlier nowhere just like you. It doesn't concern you much. After all, it's still the sixth page. You will wonder how many people even go there. But what you will fail to realize, at this point, is that you are still nowhere on search engines' result pages but your competitor who was once anonymous is now on the sixth page. He has already covered a long journey from the anonymous stage to becoming slightly visible.

Your competitor will continue working with the digital agency to improve the visibility of his business. Now, his business is on the second page. Finally, you start getting a little worried as you start seeing that business more often on the internet and start hearing about it from your current and potential customers. When the fear of loss of your customers to your competitors kicks in, you decide to hire an expert SEO agency yourself.

In this case, you have already given a very big head start to your competitor. The struggle is going to be tough and now it will need more than just SEO to win those customers.

That's why I'd recommend to always start early and take your competitors very seriously. If your competitor is doing something, you should also look into it. If you find some useful insight but you see that your competitor is still not doing that, then use that as an opportunity to strengthen your position.

- Never Stop Learning from Your Competitors

Many businesses do competitive analysis when they are launching their businesses. Once that phase is over, they completely forget about it. But this is not something that can take a backseat, this is something that needs to be constantly analyzed so nothing comes as a shock to you.

The crucial part of running any kind of successful business is to keep an eye on your competitors, watch what they're doing right and what they're doing wrong. If they have done something bad, learn from their mistakes, and if they have done something right, take inspiration from their work. In no way, consider them less smart than you.

A product will always have competition. If you think you don't have any competition, investigate again before you let that error propagate. If you still think you have no competition, there can be something wrong with the way market research is conducted. You can consider involving any experienced market research company.

Understand your competition and why they're able to do the same thing better than you. What extra features, new technology, better resources do they have that are helping them produce a more competitive product than yours. There is always something and the more you spend time learning about your competition, the more powerful you will become in strategizing your business.

In 1980, when Xerox and Canon were fighting for the copier market, Canon priced its product way too low. Xerox was definitely shocked as it found it nearly impossible to make profits at that price. But Xerox continued learning about its competition and with that, it realized that Canon is using a better version of technology for this and that's how they were competing on the basis of price.[27]

- ## Don't Compete Against Market Leaders if You Lack Resources

When you're starting a new project, try not to compete with the market leaders directly in case you don't have enough resources. As they can bury your voice easily with more marketing and advertising. If you make your product better, they can make their product far more interesting. You will be stuck in a situation where many of your customers will start moving to big market leaders because of their cheaper prices or added convenience.

In the beginning, your goal is to start earning revenue, so you don't end up depleting your cash flow. Once you have some kind of source for money coming in every month, then you can take bigger steps like thinking about expanding your market or making your product a little different.

The best you can do is to launch your product as a niche product in the market. This way you're not directly competing with the market leaders. You're just targeting a small subset of their audience if those big market players fall into your category of competition.

In case you want to open another retail ecommerce company like Amazon, you can't compete with them with similar products. The prices, the convenience of return, refunds, and various other things are way too competitive in their case. What you can do is launch an ecommerce store just for handmade furniture or handmade dresses for women.

Even if you are trying to target the niche market, the importance of differentiation can't be overlooked. This is very crucial for your business - your unique selling point. What is it that makes you different from others? We already have many dress sellers, furniture sellers, cosmetic sellers and you don't want to be just another face in that crowd.

- Don't Compete Against Yourself

When you promise but don't deliver, you start competing against yourself, against the image that you have built of your brand for your customers. Customers are very unforgiving when this happens. It's better to promise what you can easily deliver. This way your customers won't feel cheated or lied to.

If you want to safeguard your business against your own self, you have to learn what can lead to business failure and why. If there are differences between your products and your competitors' products, don't hide but use those differences to bring your audiences focus to your other strengths.

Don't compete on the basis of your weakness just because your competitors are using that particular attribute to get their message across. Your product is different from the competing products. Think about that one thing that makes you stand out from them. Once you know that, start focusing on it. This way you will be presenting a truer picture to your audience and in return will appreciate your honesty.

In any event, your message needs to be clear and consistent everywhere. Many times, false promises are made because of ineffective marketing and advertising plans. Sometimes, just to attract the customers, a wrong message is being shown but when they come looking for what they were promised, they find themselves misled.

Everything including your branding has to reinforce your message about your product.

- See the Full Picture of Your Business

Having tunnel vision and not an all-around focus on all the factors that can affect your business in some way or another can have pernicious effects. Don't ignore anything or anyone just because that seems like an insignificant risk to you. The art of a successful business lies in identifying and mitigating the risk. Not overlooking and avoiding the risk.

Fearing a competition is okay, but what is not okay is not making yourself strong enough to face that fear. Having no competition is a totally misguided and harmful kind of view. It lets you live in this dream world where everything is perfect and when you face the reality, you find yourself shocked and even worse, unprepared.

Most of the time there is going to be competition. Even if after reading this chapter you feel like you don't have competition, then there may be something wrong which can be a warning sign for your business.

One possibility can be that you are targeting a very small market. There are chances that you won't find enough customers here to sustain a profitable business model. In a case like that, you have to include more sets of people to increase your target market.

Another possibility can be that your product is way advanced for the time. Maybe you are trying to launch underwater travelling cars which sounds like a great idea but maybe many are still not there yet to think of it as a safe way to travel. There have been many such products in the last two decades which failed mainly because the audience of those times were not able to see the value in it which we do now.

The last possibility can be that you're actually working on a product that nobody wants. It seems strange to accept but if that market is wide open and it seems like a great market, then chances are there that somebody else has done the research or tried a demo product, but the audience was not very enthusiastic about it.

In either case, it will be very much advised that you double or even triple your marketing research efforts as you want to be sure that you are going to invest your time and energy in the right direction.

- Learn More About Your Customers

The key to fighting and surviving the competition lies in understanding your customers' needs. It is only then when somebody is able to satisfy their needs much better than yours, that they pick another product over yours.

So, if you don't want them to consider other competing products, you have to give them a solid reason to stick to yours. With the reason being how good you know them. What kind of needs have your products fulfilled and what still remains unmet?

Do you think you can work on them and make your product perfect? If not, do you think your competitors' products have those features that your customers are looking for which you don't have? Is it really important or is it just an additional or decorative kind of feature? How will you justify the absence of those features?

Most of the businesses still don't know much about their customers, they don't have much data and even if they have, they are not using it to refine their decision making and strategy making processes.

- Keep Innovating

You will never have to worry about your competition as long as you research and keep innovating in tune with the findings of your research. Being stagnant in a business is the death of a business. No product can survive in its original form for too long. Time changes and we change according to that. We don't have the same fashion anymore, or food choices or shopping needs. We do so much of our tasks on our laptop and our phones. We use technology for everything, and this shows the importance of continuing innovation.

What we were yesterday, we are not today and what we are going to be tomorrow, we are not today. We don't know if we are going to use the same kind of laptop that we're using right now. We don't know what kind of new advanced world we are building but all we know is that we are ready for a change that makes our society much better for us and other generations to come.

Running a business is meant for the brave hearts like you and me. It is risky but it is also rewarding if you plan and strategize well. You can't build a business environment where your product will be the sole product, and luckily you don't even want that kind of situation. By being a business owner, you are not allowed to believe in fairies.

Competition helps you to be innovative and innovation is what keeps us going and moving from one civilization to another advanced civilization.

References

27.https://businesstown.com/shows/competitive-intelligence/breaking-competition-case-study/

CHAPTER 13

Failure to Overcome Financial Hurdles

"Empty pockets never held anyone back. Only empty heads and empty hearts can do that." -Norman Vincent Peale

The Story of Short Sightedness

Once there was a construction start-up in Michigan. The start-up was very well differentiated and launched with many hopes and expectations. They had secured enough funding from the banks as well. They had devoted a chunk of those funds for marketing and advertising. Everything was great but there was only one problem that led to their downfall.

According to their company policy, a client was supposed to make a payment of 20% upfront and 80% at the time of project completion. Many of those projects lasted for more than two months. What happened as a result? There was more cash going out in the form of employee salaries and operational costs but not enough cash coming in which could have made it easier to continue operating every month without any issue. With that, they were stuck in a situation where there was more cash flowing out than in.

Soon, they couldn't afford any kind of marketing because marketing companies needed money in advance, and they were getting cash tied. Then, employees' salaries started getting delayed. It became a normal statement that their dues would be cleared as soon as they receive the money from their clients. Eventually, the cash flow problem became too bad and couldn't sustain their own business model. Thus, they went out of the business.

Lack of Funds

What are the building blocks of a business?

1. An experienced and skilled team to bring your idea to life.
2. The latest technology to make your business operate faster and more efficient.
3. Marketing and advertising so you are heard, seen and loved by your audience.
4. Various types of equipment for operating an office. Even if you move to a virtual office, you will still need a lot of things to run your business.

If you are an eCommerce business owner, you will be investing a major portion of your funds in a warehouse, production unit, raw material, marketing and advertising so your audience knows you have something to offer. If you're a restaurant owner, you will be investing a lot in building a kitchen, good seating area, ambient lighting, chefs, food, and marketing and advertising to build a customer base.

If you're a hotel owner, you will be required to put your funds in a good location, hotel staff training, various amenities that you want to provide to your guests - swimming pool, gym, linens, furniture, spa, hotel restaurant, marketing and advertising so you can fill your hotel with guests.

Let's say you're a healthcare business owner. Now, you will put your funds in high-tech healthcare devices, experienced doctors, staff members, marketing and advertising so you can build and maintain a good reputation and build strong doctor-patient relationships.

In short, whatever business you own or decide to own in the future, you will need a significant amount of funds to invest. To make sure you don't run out of your funds before your business starts generating a profit, you need to practice caution on how you plan to spend your limited money.

Depleting funds without being replenished is the number one cause for business failure.

According to research by the U.S. Bank, 50% of the businesses fail within five years and 82% of the time the reason is poor cash flow. [29]

Money Mistakes to Avoid

- ## Starting A Business Without Proper Funds to Back It Up

    As cited on the Counselors to America's Small Business, 79% of the businesses start with way too little money than required for sustaining that business.[27] The reason why so many people start a business without enough money is because they are being overly optimistic. They think they will be able to make profits sooner than other similar businesses in the industry.

    However, they end up losing grip on reality as their views get blurred by extreme optimism. I am not asking you to stop being optimistic, I am asking you to get realistic and optimistic at the same time.

Do not take extreme decisions after completing a self-help book. Take a deep breath. Think about it from every angle. If you want, brainstorm with your business partners and then decide.

Don't deny facts and numbers. If the numbers are saying that within six months you will run out of money if you don't break even, then you need to take that seriously. Start by figuring out if there is a way you can achieve that within six months or sooner than that. If not, is there a way you can secure some kind of investment? If not, what are your other options? If, after all the brainstorming, you realize that the minimum time to break even for your business will be a year and you also don't have any other investment sources, then starting a business is not a great idea.

- Investing Funds in Wrong Areas

The expression, "People don't plan to fail, they just fail to plan" sounds very accurate when it comes to figuring out where to invest. A lot of business owners have invested their money in various unnecessary fields. I had once worked with a consultant who owned an office triple the size of what she actually needed because it looked cool.

In another case, I've worked with an entrepreneur who loved investing his funds for the office decoration. Even though he didn't have a business model where customers were required to walk into the office, the company's management invested most of their money in getting a fancy, oversized office in the most expensive location and latter in beautifying it.

Only 10% of the office was full, the rest always remained empty. It was so empty that you could hear the sound of money being emptied in the echoes.

Compared to this, their budget for promotion of their services was only 1% of their total budget which they had kept decreasing after every month.

Did I mention there was wide unrest among employees because they were not getting any promotions, salary raises or any kind of bonus? The office continued getting fancier and the promotion continued to get smaller. The result was many employees felt dissatisfied and didn't contribute their one hundred percent. In addition, the turnover rate was sky rocketing, and no action was ever taken to improve the situation. On the bright side, the office looked pretty.

This is a classic example of misallocation of funds. What do you think happened afterward? Unable to see the results, the motivation of the founder and the team had died and with that, the project came to an end. Plus, unhappy employees also started quitting.

As soon as an employee decides to leave your company, all the investment of time, energy and money you have put in boarding and training that employee goes to waste.

As can be seen, poor cash planning leads to a loss of investment.

.

- Choosing Short Term Benefits Over Long Term Gains

This is actually a very common mistake that many entrepreneurs have made in the past and some are making even right now. We always become attracted to short term benefits and that's why we spend a major portion of our money on it. Instead of digital advertising, we fix our websites twenty times because we can see a well-designed website right away, but we can't see the results of digital advertising so soon.

In other cases, we invest a lot of resources in making a video ad for our products but then we decide against prompting it.

Similarly, it takes a considerable amount of investment when it comes to building a brand but is it worth it? Let's ask Nike and Coke! When we start the process of branding, we generally don't notice much of a difference instantly, not even in a year. It's possible to even feel like your investment is not bringing you any sales.

Ultimately, you will decide to route your funds in some other fast result-generating areas and will never reach a stage of becoming the Nike of your industry.

The issue is not just related to branding, but it extends to every area of marketing. Marketing is an investment that generally generates long term results. For example, if you invest in SEO, you won't see your website on the first page of Google search results in a month. It will take at least a year, but that doesn't reduce the importance of working on it. The results of this marketing activity may bloom late but they are still helpful.

Investing in things that will give you long term growth is always a good idea.

The same goes for the field of market research, you might not see the results straight away, but they are there. Knowing your audience well as a part of the market research will pay off with improved customer loyalty and relationship building.

- ## Inability to Control Expenses

In the end, invest your funds in the right activities. Also, make sure that all your money is not locked in. You have to invest and then make money so you can invest again. And this cycle continues. If you don't have easy cash flow, you will get stuck and will soon be out of cash.

Plan, plan and plan a little more!

Do you think you have to go to extremes to learn the value of proper planning of how to use your funds? I think not. You don't want to lose your money. Not only will it affect your current project but will also decrease your possibility of starting something new.

I will say the biggest skill you can develop, as a business owner, is learning from the mistakes of others and never repeating them.

Afterall, the mistakes in a business world are costly, time consuming and deadly. As a result, the more that you polish your skill of learning from others' mistakes, the more you will be able to put your funds to the right use.

Learning from Other's Mistakes

I have known a lot of business owners. Many of them used their funds wisely, many have not. Many are still in business and growing while many others have disappeared from the market. Here's why many of the businesses failed:

- ## Inability to Secure Financing

    If you don't have the initial capital to start your business, you will become dependent on the external sources in order to do so. Gaining funds though secondary sources is not so easy as the market is highly competitive and the amount of funds available are also limited.

    First and foremost, you'll need funds from somebody other

than your parents which will contribute to your business idea and business plan. A strong business idea with a profitable future will no doubt attract better financing rather than the other options. After your idea, your financial statements become very crucial for deciding your business' future. Unrealistic profit projections are not going to win you the trust of your investors.

- Inability to Build a Realistic Budget

I can't tell you how often I have seen people overestimate their revenue and profits and underestimate their expenses. What happens when reality strikes them? They'll listen to the song Yesterday by The Beatles on repeat.

That's why, you need to build a budget which is not just accurate but can also help you through tough times without burning all your cash down.

It's good to overestimate your expenses but not your revenue. This way when you are left with extra profit, you will be happily surprised instead of shocked when you see negative cash. The importance of budget making lies in the fact that you need to first analyze how you want to spend that money before you can start earning it.

This will help you in understanding how many months you can last without any revenue, how much marketing budget you can afford, how many employees you can have, and what the price of your product or services should be. Without a budget, you will not have any clue about any of your expenses and how much money you need to earn to pay off those expenses plus save a little more which you can invest into your business again.

A realistic budget will tell you how much money you have, how much can you spend and how much more you have to bring in every year to continue being in the business. A realistic budget will also significantly cut down your risks to your business.

- Misallocation of Budget

In one of the stories that I've shared above, you can see that the reason for their business' downfall was their misallocation of budget. Marketing, advertising, technology, promotions, operations, supply chain management, recruiting and office management: you will be doing a lot of multitasking. It gets confusing sometimes to figure out how to allocate money to all these areas in the best possible way.

One important thing that you have to remember is that the human brain is always looking for instant gratification and instant results which is why many of us end up spending more budget on making our office or store prettier rather than on marketing.

This is also the reason why we hire low-paying unqualified professionals over high-paying qualified ones because the instant saving brings us pleasure. Unfortunately, we forget about the bad performance of those employees and their effect on the business outcomes at that time.

We don't like delayed responses, but businesses aren't meant to be short-term.

Businesses are long-term investments. Just like your stock investments. You can't invest in the market and think in a month, you will become a millionaire. You wait for years and years to build that money but in the end, you feel delighted that you've made that decision. The difference between short-term benefits and long-term benefits are like building a nice office versus building a brand like Coca Cola. If you are not going to invest in the long-term growth of your company in the form of marketing, then you can't expect that in five or ten years, you will become a known brand.

- Misuse of Budget

What happens when the business budget is misused? What happens when we give our top management and ourselves unjustifiable hefty salaries and various other perks? The business suffers the losses.

Just like the one hundred-million-dollar home design start-up known as Homepolish collapsed because of the misuse of the budget by its founders. They more than doubled their salaries within a short period of time.[30]

Misuse of budget happens when business owners are not able to see far ahead in the future or don't take the budget seriously. So often we ignore the discrepancies in our budget because we find them to be very small but these discrepancies when added becomes huge and impacts the budget badly. This problem can be solved if we start observing our budget once it is planned and implemented. We are doing it so we can catch any discrepancy right on time before it becomes a huge gap which becomes tough to be filled.

- Lack of Cash Flow

Poor cash flow management is the major reason why businesses fail. If your expenses exceed your revenue, then it means you are having a cash flow problem. When you launch a business, it's understandable that your expenses are going to be higher. You will be required to invest a lot in marketing, promotion, sales, setting up your store and various other things but eventually your revenue needs to rise. If they still don't, even after some time, then you're going to be stuck in a vicious cycle of business failure due to the decrease of funds every passing month.

To have a working capital, your business assets should be higher than your business liabilities. It's also very much dependent on your accounts receivable. Here's what I mean by that.

Let's say your customers pay you after two months of purchasing a service or product but payments for business expenses need to be done in fifteen days. In a case like that, you will have to pay cash in fifteen days, but you are getting cash in sixty days. This implies that you will be out of cash soon if you continue doing it. This is going to hurt your available working capital for even other business activities like planning, procuring raw materials and marketing.

- Financial Illiteracy

This is another important reason for business failure. Many times, inexperienced entrepreneurs and bloggers start their business without fully understanding the importance of proper financial planning and management. Many times, they base their decisions just on their gut feeling, without considering any numbers. They fail to see how much money they are spending every month and how much time it will take to bring the money in.

Without any numbers, they are just guessing that they will be able to make revenues in a few months. But when they prepare a budget, check all the numbers, and understand the market, they realize that it will take more than a few months to just break even.

If they still decide to go into the industry, they can plan efficiently according to their current situation. In case they run out of cash before they start getting cash in, all the budget planning will help them in knowing how far away they are from the goal. If there's a little gap, they can figure something out.

Another thing that financial illiteracy can lead to is inefficient spending. You may end up spending money on decorating your store when you need marketing to increase awareness or you may end up hiring high-salaried employees when at the moment you can only afford interns or you may end up buying an office triple the size you need just because it looks good.

- Expansion of Business Before You Are Ready

When a business is expanded, we have to do many things again from scratch. For example, we will need to build a new store or office in that location, hire and train new employees to handle the extended market, increase the budget for marketing to cover the new area, pay for various utilities and many other things.

You will face a lot of challenges that you've faced when you started the first branch of your business. Not to forget, your money will be locked in again for some time. This implies you won't be able to generate revenues from your new business right away. There will be a cash flow outside but not inside.

So, you can expand your business only if you have enough budget to afford such kind of cash flow. If you can't afford locking your money in expansion for a few months without generating revenue, then you should wait until you have enough cash.

Securing funds is the first step but managing those funds efficiently and effectively is the most crucial step for your business' survival as well as growth. If investors have just approved some capital, remember that it's just the first step.

References

28.https://www.businessinsider.com/why-small-businesses-fail-infographic-2017-8?r=US&IR=T

29.https://www.preferredcfo.com/cash-flow-reason-small-businesses-fail/

30.https://marker.medium.com/how-homepolishs-extremely-instagrammable-house-of-cards-came-tumbling-down-d7a7d1780ddc

CHAPTER 14

Failure to Build an Employee Team

"None of us is as smart as all of us." -Ken Blanchard

The Story of Discontent

Employees of a company need to be bound together with love and respect, and not by dissatisfaction and helplessness. This statement came to life in one of the companies of San Diego. Every single employee in this company was highly dissatisfied. There was no HR department, and neither the senior management was interested in understanding and dealing with employee problems.

There was no training program, no motivation, no appreciation, not even a promotion after years of hard work. Everyone was dissatisfied. People were leaving the company left and right leaving bad reviews everywhere. Whoever stayed with the company stayed because they were helpless.

When senior management was not around, employees talked about how dissatisfied they were with the company. One time, it was proposed to improve the company image as it had too many bad reviews. The image improvement project included feedback from the employees and working on the issues.

Do you know what happened after that? The senior management asked if there is a way that we can remove their complaints rather than having a discussion with the employees to work on their issues.

What they had failed to realize in all this is, **"Employee loyalty is cheaper than hiring new employees, training them, and motivating them."**

This entire process of employee onboarding takes a lot of time and energy. In the end, **if your employees are happy, they become your salespeople who speak with utmost passion for the company they work for.** Thus, transferring the same emotion and passion in the potential customers.

There's one more story for you. This was a software company in New Jersey. This time the company was bigger, and there was even an HR department. But still a lot was missing this time. Often the HR department and the direct managers will change the company policies as per their convenience. Leave policies, notice period, appraisal policies - everything was different according to every employee. Not in documents but in practice. This led to unfair policies and created the discontent among the employees.

In one case, an employee will not get his leave approved to visit his sick mom while in another case, an employee will be allowed on leave to see a baseball match. The company had good days following these unfair policies before the advent of the digital age. But once the internet became popular, what was going on in the company started coming to light. More and more employees started talking about their experiences on social media, reviewing platforms, and discussion portals like Reddit and it completely hurt their business.

A discontent employee means not getting the results 100% and the loss of a company advocate as well.

How an Employee Team is Built?

Building an employee team or employee tribe is a little time consuming which requires little effort but in the long process of achieving business growth, it's totally worth it.

Employee tribe consists of a group of employees who are equally as passionate about your idea just like you, who love working with you and also believe in you. Such a team is very powerful and capable of achieving wondrous results. Here's how you can build your own employee tribe:

- ## Hiring a Superstar

    The first step of your employee tribe starts with hiring the superstar out of all the applicants. Hiring is not as simple as you think. You have to make sure you are hiring somebody who is going to be a great fit in the kind of employee tribe you're building.

    Focus on how applicants' values match your company's values. If the values don't match, you won't be able to instill the right amount of passion in them and without passion, there won't be any employee tribe.

    However, don't ever hire a yes man. Do you remember the story of the emperor's new clothes? If not, here's the summary for you. An emperor shows off his new clothes when in reality, he is wearing none. But everyone around him is too scared to tell him that, so they all pretend and praise his new clothes. You don't want to be that emperor.

    I know it feels good when people agree with what you're saying. That ego boost by being right! When it comes to business, it's so much better to be corrected when you're wrong rather than being applauded for your wrong ideas. It can save a business from a downfall. I was once a part of a team like that. The CEO had a very unrealistic idea and expectation from his idea. He kept talking about how all the people who are going to visit the website will sign up to become a part of their product community. When did that ever happen?

The percentage of people taking a desired action on your website is 4.31%. In case it's an ecommerce website, it's around 2.63%.[31] If we look at these numbers, having an expectation that 100% of the people will do what you want them to do on your website is totally wrong. Not everyone is going to like what you're offering. Some will need more convincing. Some will sign up and will unsubscribe later.

Interestingly, nobody ever mentioned this to the CEO that a 100% satisfaction rate has never been achieved in history. There is no perfect product in the world and there will never be. I didn't mention for a few days when I had found everyone around me agreeing with his wrong expectations but finally, I had to tell the senior management that this is not realistic.

What happened after that?

Many senior managers agreed with me but when the time came to tell the CEO, they backed out as they didn't want to make him unhappy and hurt their chances of promotion. The business owner didn't like my realistic views and numbers. I just lost my chances of promotion, but the company lost their chances of growth.

- Training

Many business owners think that their work is over once the employee has joined the company but in reality, the work is just getting started. One of the companies I'd worked for didn't invest in any kind of training program at all but without that, employees are not able to sharpen their skills.

Today, we use so many different kinds of software and tools in every profession and they aren't constant. Even if your employees know one tool, let's say one particular Customer Relationship Management software, they will still need training as in a few years a newer version will be launched, or a new tool will replace the existing one.

In addition, different kinds of training are really helpful in improving the efficiency of a business. Training looks like a financial loss to many but when your employees learn something new and implement the same for your company, they improve efficiency of your business process which gives you a competitive edge. Isn't that what we all need to survive?

We all have been very impressed with Starbucks and McDonald's services. Everything seems smooth at these places and also, consistent wherever you go. Their employees are not from similar backgrounds and still somehow, they all exhibit the same style. Employees learn about the importance of consistency and quality control through their training program.

Imagine your employees as your kids, now it's your turn to nurture them, instill your brand value in them and turn them into your loyal team members.

Investing in your employees seems like a waste of money but it's not. When your employees learn new and advanced ways of doing something, they are going to apply it to your company. Thus, making the efficiency and productivity of your company go higher.

When you invest in your employees' development, they'll

spend their skills in your company's development.

If you think there is a new marketing tool out there, organize a training program for your marketing department, if you see there is a new way of identifying the right candidate, organize a training program for your HR team. Let the training never stop.

If you won't train them, you will be the only one who knows of the new tools and new process and then, either you will be spending most of your time doing all the work by yourself or will be spending a lot of your time trying to fix the mistakes your employees made because they didn't receive any training in those areas where you excel.

- Motivation and Productivity Improvement
Salary is not the motivation! Big surprise! It's true.

Many business owners think that they are paying a salary to their employees and that should be enough motivation for them to want to work harder. But humans are not as simple and why would we be? We are not bots whose behavior can be predicted. We are humans, we are more complex, we are more emotional.

We need constant care. We need appreciation, recognition, promotion, respect, safety and a lot more. And that's why you have to invest your time in understanding your employees. You can bring out the best in them by learning about what motivates them.

- Employee Tribe Building
By now, you have invested your time in training and motivating your employees but the process doesn't end there. You also need to build a team.

A team is built when your employees are inspired by the

same vision and connected with the same goal.

If we say that our office is like our second home. Then, our team should be like our second family.

Building a family is tough but who could deny the happiness of having people by our side when things don't go as we plan.

A team is not built when there are independent and clashing HR, sales, marketing, finance or any other department's goals, but a team is built when they all work together toward achieving the same goal.

The first and the only rule of team building is employees being comfortable with each other. That comfort comes when they know each other, when they can easily ask each other whatever they want, when they are not weighed down by the roles of seniority, when they are not treated as paid employees but as equal partners in the growth of the company.

Everyone is contributing to the same goal. It doesn't only apply to the sales team, IT team, finance team or any other team - they all contribute and that's how you reach a new stage. For that reason, remember when you share the credit of your growth, don't just praise one team and build discontent in another just because you've failed to see how indirectly their efforts led to the achievement of final goals.

- Loyalty Development

A person becomes a loyal member when they find something in a company that they were longing for but couldn't find it. It can be anything.

It can be as simple as recognition for their work, love of other team members, acceptance by the team, or respect for their ideas. Loyalty development is tied to motivation, if you know what motivates an employee, you will be able to turn that into loyalty development.

Mistakes to Avoid While Building an Employee Team

Your employees shouldn't be scared of being let go but you should be scared of them leaving you.

Unfortunately, we see it the other way around. We always think, as a business owner, we have the power to pull the strings whenever we want. But we don't! How much does it cost when a good employee decides to leave you? A lot! All the hiring, training and motivation cost. Plus, now you have to spend the same time again in training another one which pushes your project even farther away from the its completion date. If it was supposed to be finished in a year, you know you might need another three to four months to bring the new trainee at the same stage where the previous employee was, making your project deadline 1.4 years. Unfortunately, there are no prenups in the business world.

Here are a few mistakes that we make that we should try to avoid:

- ## Failure to Build a Thriving Environment

   A good work culture and work environment is very crucial in helping your employees to put their best foot forward. If the environment is not right, they will not be able to give their 100%. A work environment becomes counter-productive if it is filled with dissatisfaction, negativity, unresolved complaints, and desire to win at the cost of others.

   You need an environment where your employees are not afraid to share even their silliest ideas. A place where they are respected, loved and heard, where they feel like an important part of the team.

- Micromanaging

A boss lurking behind you to look into your computer to know what you're doing, a boss asking every day to share a report on what you're working on, monitoring your emails and a lot more, these are all the signs that you are micromanaged by your manager.

This is a part of a toxic environment. Your employees will never flourish in an environment like that. They want to not be spied on all the time. They want some kind of autonomy on the project and independence of executing the project in their own way.

Your task should be to share the goals and some important instructions related to your brand image, rest how that project needs to be executed so that the goals are met is going to be your employees' task now. You have to learn to leave them alone and give them a deadline and check on the assigned deadline the progress of the project. Don't ask every day, "Where's the report now?"

A long time ago, I also had a similar boss who loved micromanaging. Every day he would ask, "What did you do today? How far has the project progressed?"

And it kept becoming weirder and weirder because as a marketer, sometimes we spend days just thinking of a perfect strategy to reach the goals. It's not expected that the idea will pop in anyone's head in just a day. But I knew that my boss wouldn't understand if I had sent him a status update that for the past three days I'm trying to think of a new idea or a strategy. In this case, because of micromanaging I was not able to have enough time to come up with a ground-breaking marketing idea.

- ## Failure to Create an Effective Chain of Communication

Effective two-way communication is responsible for building the trust in a company and keeping the employees happy. Your employees want to know what's happening with the project, and how their work is contributing to the project.

Even more, when they are easily able to get their ideas across to the senior management, they feel encouraged and come up with even more ideas. Some of them can actually be amazing. Also, it helps them in getting their grievances redressed and share their feedback with the responsible authority easily.

- ## Lack of Transparency and Trust

Transparency comes in a project when you start treating your employees as your equals, as your business partners rather than mere salaried employees.

Transparency when things are going well and even when things are going bad, keeps all your employees in the chain which makes them feel connected to the project even more.

- ## Disagreements and Handling of Disagreements

Disagreements are unavoidable, but how you handle them can make all the difference. There can be disagreements among two employees, two teams and even you and your employees. There is a right way of handling this and then there is an ego-boosting way. We all know that the second one is not as amazing as it sounds.

When you boost your own ego because you don't want to

be termed wrong by your juniors, you are just feeding your ego which will help you feel good only in that moment, but it might not help you or your project in the long run.

You need to be respectful of others' ideas even if they don't match yours. You have to listen to others and if they are wrong, you have to still be respectful. You can give constructive feedback and explain why a particular idea doesn't seem like a good idea to you.

However, if you're wrong, you have to be willing to accept that you didn't get to see the problem in a way your employee does. It's commendable and you will think more about it.

Most of the time, you're not on the same wavelength as your employees when you both have different goals. Maybe you're thinking of your own personal goals rather than the shared company goals. It can be the other way around as well, so you have to make sure that you all have to be at the same wavelengths if you want to keep the disagreements low and productivity high.

The Aftermath of Hiring Wrong or Incompetent Professionals

As a business owner, many times we're so consumed in the task of perfecting our product for our customers, that we forget to perfect our team. The importance of a good team is still not understood by many. You can start a business, but that business can only be pushed forward by a team of expert professionals.

Which is Worse - Hiring the Wrong Employee or Firing That Employee Way Too Late?

The Real Cost of a Bad Apple

We all make wrong hiring decisions at least once in our professional lives. Sometimes we have a low budget, so we try to adjust with whoever is willing to work in that amount. Other times we don't have enough time and we hire the first candidate we like. Not just that, nepotism can also severely affect our businesses.

There are many other reasons why we make bad hiring decisions. Perhaps understanding how these bad decisions affect our businesses will help us in minimizing the number of bad apples in the future.

- Productivity is Affected

    The effects of wrong hiring can be seen for many years. When an unfit, unskilled or incompetent person joins a team, the project instead of moving forward starts moving backward. In a situation like that, all the team members are now burdened with this extra responsibility of not just finishing their own tasks on time but to also make sure that the project does not become stagnant by picking up the person's slack. This, in turn, will burn them out which will soon start reflecting in the progress of the project.

    When that same wrong person is let go, the situation doesn't improve immediately. It leads to the disruption of the project. In addition, the morale of your team also goes down with that. When morale goes down, so does the productivity. Poor performers bring the standard of work down. Poor performance and disengagement from work are very contagious. If one person performs badly, then the others won't have enough motivation to perform much better than they formerly had.

When I had started my company, I made the same mistake. I'd hired many wrong employees because I didn't have enough time. The first few good profiles I saw, I hired them. It took me a few months to hire them, it took me another few months to train them, and then it took me another few months to bring the morale of my team up again after letting them go.

This entire situation affected my work drastically. I was more consumed by management tasks than the launching of the project itself. I had tried for some time to get them back on track but in the end, I've realized that letting them go was one of the best decisions I have ever made for my business.

- ## Wrong Decision Making

A company doesn't grow based off the work of one person, it grows when many people work together as a team toward the same shared goal. One thing we should never forget is that the work of all the employees in a company depends on each other. What one does will affect another.

A team is very much like a chain. The weakest link in the chain will affect the entire strength of that chain.

Who doesn't remember the saying that we are as strong as the weakest link in the chain? If one person makes a mistake and if that mistake is not corrected on time, it leads to another mistake and then another mistake and soon we have a big disaster waiting for us.

Let's imagine you've hired a social media manager who isn't very skilled. He wrongly interprets the social media data and presents that inaccurate data to your IT manager. Now, your IT manager is going to decide the next steps for the team based on the wrong data presented. The situation will not improve at any point but will keep escalating.

For example, an expert marketing team will help you make a decision in the right direction. An incompetent marketing team will only move you farther away from your business goal. The same goes for all the other teams and members who make those teams. That's why you should never let one team's wrong decisions feed into another's team's decision making, thus creating a snowball effect.

- ## Financial Loss

Zappos CEO once said that wrong hiring has led to a loss of over $100 million for their company.[32] This is not a small number. When a wrong hiring decision is made, we lose our hiring, training and development time and cost.

The bigger the company is, the bigger the financial effects of such hiring will be. Smaller companies risk more than that when they hire someone. They risk their future because small businesses and start-ups have limited time and also limited money. Limited time because their competitors can outrun them if they take too long. Not to mention, if they spend a lot of their money in just the hiring, training, firing, and rehiring process, they will soon run out of money for other business-related functions which will take them out of the business world.

We can't completely eliminate the chances of hiring somebody wrong. It is very much like dating.

All we can do is avoid hiring anyone based on the wrong reasons.

We shouldn't try to get emotional while hiring. We should also not try to fill a position hastily. Remember that you are building a team of all those people who should love your idea as much as you do. Building a strong team like that takes resources but it will be one of the best decisions you will ever make.

References

31.   https://www.invespcro.com/blog/the-average-website-conversion-rate-by-industry/
32.   http://www.businessinsider.com/tony-hsieh-making-the-right-hires-2010-10

CHAPTER 15

Poor Customer Service and Client Success Strategy

"A brand for a company is like a reputation for a person. You earn reputation by trying to do hard things well." - Jeff Bezos

The Story of Inconvenience

This is the story of a grocery store in San Diego. They had a physical store for many years, but they recently made the decision to move their business online as well. People loved going to their brick and mortar location but unfortunately, people didn't show the same response for their online store/website. Instead of investigating the reason, they'd assumed that the internet sales were ineffective when it comes to groceries and also the marketing was not done properly. But what they didn't realize was that internet selling works great for groceries. This is how Amazon became big.

Their marketing was effective, but marketing doesn't run a business alone. The problem with their online venture was that they were unable to translate their physical store customer service into their online store convenience.

In their physical store, there was a staff member who had helped customers with returns and refunds. This entire process was very smooth and fast, but it was cumbersome if done online. Most of the customer emails went unanswered. And in case they were answered, it took almost two to three weeks in this process. As a result, customer satisfaction started decline. They'd felt they were not heard, and nobody even attempted to solve their issues.

The company thought that they could ignore the online business issues and concentrate on just their physical store. But it doesn't work that way. Soon, many of the satisfied customers who had bad experiences on the store website started switching to other businesses with better online customer service. This way the side effects of poor online customer service started reflecting even in the physical store and soon they were stripped of a big chunk of their satisfied and loyal customers.

From a profitable business, it turned into a merely surviving business. Very soon, they started rethinking everything and decided to get all their issues fixed. Then, they contacted us, and we provided them with a customer strategy which helped both their online and offline channels flourish, without prioritizing one over the other.

Why Do You Need a Good Customer Service and Client Success Strategy?

The answer to this is very simple. You need a good customer service and client success strategy because it helps your business grow. If you have any other goal from your business apart from this, then you can skip this chapter. But if you want to grow and not just stay stagnate in one place, you need good customer service. Here's some other reasons why you should start focusing on it:

- ## Loyalty is Highly Profitable

  Acquiring new customers takes a lot of time, effort and a considerable amount of your marketing budget. But retaining the old customers doesn't take much - just listening to their problems. By the way, also works in marriage. This is the easiest way you can gain a customer.

  Customers' lifelong value as compared to how much marketing budget you have spent in getting them is much lower compared to getting a new customer and then losing that customer because of your poor marketing strategy.

- ## Reduces Your Marketing Budget

  A good marketing can't overcome your poor customer strategy, but a good customer service can compensate for your poor marketing. There is no version of marketing, how much you are willing to pay, that can help you replace a good customer strategy.

  So, if you want to use your marketing budget effectively and get more customers at cheaper acquisition cost, you should start working on your customer service. It costs very little and pays heavily.

- ## Builds Reputation

  As we're all aware that the digital world is full of spammers, cheaters and hackers. Trusting anyone with your bank details is not an easy task for anyone. That's why, I recommend my clients to start focusing on building their reputation equity in addition to their financial equity, brand equity and customer equity. This is something that we deeply believe and follow at Bizadmark.

If you have an impeccable reputation on the internet, more and more people are going to trust you.

When you are trusted, customers will feel comfortable when buying from you because they know that their bank details are safe with you as you have their best interest in mind.

Once their trust grows stronger, reputation is built. And in the digital age, reputation is more expensive than anything.

The internet has made our businesses more fragile than they were ever before. You can lose your reputation easily with one wrong tweet, one wrong image and one wrong post. So, start paying more attention to your digital customer strategy. You don't want any of your online actions to take a hit on your brand reputation.

Customers can share negative reviews if your customer strategy is not good. Sharing reviews and letting others know how you feel about a product has never been so easy as it is now. People love to share their experiences through social media channels.

Social media is a place where customers' positive posts about your brand can bring you free publicity. However, their negative posts can damage your reputation and cost you many customers. These reviews influence many people every day. After reading somebody else' negative review, people change their mind of doing business with a brand even without checking out their website or knowing about their brand.

"It takes twenty years to build a reputation and five minutes to ruin it. If you think about that, you'll do things differently." - Warren Buffett

- Attracts New Customers

A good customer strategy will make your current customers happy which will reflect in their reviews. These reviews influence many people every day. A good word shared online will bring so many more new customers.

Online word-of-mouth is very powerful. These days customer service is one of the most important differentiation factors used by customers to pick one brand over others.

Let's say two brands have identical services. Or maybe one brand has slightly better products than the other one. Who do you think customers are going to prefer? The answer is the one who is going to have better customer service, not the one who has a slightly better product.

So, start working on your customer success strategy and make it one of your unique selling propositions. There can't be any technique or marketing campaign that can bring you customers so easily than this one.

What Customer Mistakes Can Cost You Your Business?

It happens so often that we forget to regularly monitor our customer service strategies, but customer strategy is the only one which can't be ignored. It has to be exceptional, not just good.

For creating an exceptional customer strategy, you have to start paying attention to it more often. You have to keep an eye on your customer retention rate, customer satisfaction, and customer feedback. Plus, you should always be aware of current industry trends, so you can adapt with time.

Remember your customers appreciate efficiency and convenience and those two become achievable through innovation and willingness to change with time.

No Customer Service Strategy

An effective customer service strategy is the one which will never stop learning more about your customers. When you're trying to know more about your customers, you learn even little things about them - what your customers are doing and more importantly, why are they even doing it?

The moment you will be able to understand the hidden inner reason for their actions, you will be able to deliver exactly what they want. This will lead to improved customer satisfaction which is the most effective way of increasing your business and growing it exponentially.

On the other hand, a bad customer strategy will not only just affect your current customers but your future customers, too. You will be able to attract customers to your brand but then you will lose them in the end.

Not to mention, you won't be able to easily convert many leads into customers as they will read about your bad customer service strategy somewhere. (Nothing remains private on the internet.)

In case they don't find any negative reviews, they might experience your broken customer service, feel frustrated and post negative reviews themselves thus hurting your future sales.

Don't make customers wait in line for too long, don't put them on hold or transfer from one agent to another, don't reply to them late after many days just to make them repeat the same problem they said earlier, don't provide the chat feature if your chat can't help them, if your employees are rude, unprofessional and are not sympathizing with your customers-in-distress.

Inadequate Grievance Redressal System

Who handles all the customer complaints and how? This entire process will determine your customer satisfaction index. The process of grievance redressal is generally like this:

- A customer writes an email or calls a customer care representative to talk about the issue they had.

  Here, how much time they are required to wait before they can hear back from the company's representative is very crucial. The faster your customers hear back from you, the more they will appreciate it. They don't want to send an email to you only to be answered after a week. They don't want to call your customer care and be in a queue listening to some frustrating music for over thirty minutes.

- A customer care representative will pick up the call and answer it.

  Now, who is this representative and how well are they trained? The better the training you provide to a customer care representative, the better they will make your frustrated customers feel. Good customer care representatives will possess good knowledge to answer any questions without beating around the bush and delaying the issue for a few more days until they find somebody else to look into it. In addition, how professional your team is, is also important.

Lack of Response Time

There can be a delay in delivering value to your customers, in responding to their complaints or in solving their issues. Any kind of wait time is detrimental to your business. Your customers will not keep on waiting till you fix everything. They have an alternative. They can switch to your competitor's products or any other substitute whoever can provide them good and fast customer service.

When it comes to customer service, you are no longer competing with just your competitors, you are also competing with every business. Don't we all want every single business to start providing us the kind of service that we received from that one place we still can't stop thinking of? Don't we find ourselves thinking what will happen if everyone can deliver their products in a few hours just like Wholefoods?

Choosing Business Goals Over Customer Satisfaction

What we should never forget is that customers are our businesses. Customers and businesses are not two separate entities. They don't have two different clashing goals.

They both have the same goal set and this mutually beneficial goal will bring more growth to your business. You are not selling products. You are selling value to your customers. The more value your customers see, the more they will like your business. The more they like your business, the more they will buy. The more they buy, the more business growth you will see.

That's why, the next time you think about your business goal, stop thinking about your product, but start thinking about how you can increase the customer value.

Make your business strategy customer-centric, not product-centric, business-centric, or profit-centric. Set clear objectives and observe them regularly. As soon as you see any discrepancies, work to change those numbers and make them more favorable for your business.

Happy Customers, Unhappy Employees

The cycle of keeping your customers happy but your employees unhappy is very damaging for your business' growth. As in the end, your employees are the ones who are generating customer value, interacting with your customers and solving their problems.

If they are unhappy, their unhappiness and discontent will reflect in their actions. In addition, they won't be able to transfer the right passion and feelings for the brand in your customers, if they themselves don't feel the same way.

If you want to keep your customers happy, start by keeping your employees happy.
These small changes pay a lot in the long run.

Always keep in mind that if all of your customers are not satisfied and delighted by your services, you still have a lot of improvements to make. To look at it differently, you still have a lot of opportunities to grow your business.

Create a positive and sentimental experience for your customers. Give them reasons for turning them into lifelong customers. If you want to retain your customers, attract more customers, and don't want to unnecessarily spend your budget in marketing campaigns which will fail because of your increasing number of dissatisfied customers, start working on your customer service strategy right now.

CHAPTER 16

Ignoring the Health of Your Body and Mind

"It is health that is real wealth and not pieces of gold and silver." -Mahatma Gandhi

The Story of an Entrepreneur

This is the story of Mr. Ron Donaldson. He was working on a very good AI related idea. The idea was mind blowing and there was definitely a market for that product. Everything was going great with the business. They have done a lot of market research to understand the needs of their target audience. Additionally, they have also put aside a good enough budget for marketing and advertising activities.

Everything was going as per the plan except the mental health of Mr. Ron.

An entrepreneur goes through a tremendous amount of stress which is generally hidden behind the strong exterior of a leader. There are funds to be managed, a team to be built and clients need to be acquired within a strict time frame. If entrepreneurs are unable to achieve that, they have to see their business fall apart.

Due to this, a strong mind becomes one of the most important prerequisites for becoming an entrepreneur.

Mr. Ron has never worked under so much pressure. His entrepreneurial adventure has brought a lot of uncertainty with it. In addition, as a leader of the company, he'd worked long hours trying to figure out solutions for every issue by himself, but all those issues were affecting him. Soon, he was not able to take any more stress and he started crumbling under pressure.

He became more and more distracted, and less and less productive. His decision-making became impaired. He made a few bad decisions which impacted his business. He finally had to take a break from his business and work on his mental health first.

A Healthy Body Leads to a Healthy Mind

This isn't a typical self-help book telling you how to feel better about yourself. It's a business book and the purpose of this book is to help you in succeeding in your business. Great health is definitely something that affects your business in positive ways.

Not to mention, a healthy body leads to a healthy mind and a healthy mind is the most important tool you can have as a business owner.

When you take care of yourself, you will improve the length and quality of your life as well as increase the quality of your business and add more years to its life.

As a business owner, it's understandable that you are so short on time. However, you should never build your business at the cost of your health. When it comes to working on your current project or working out in the gym, many times you end up picking the project. I have done that as well. I have ignored many of my work out days with the excuse that the ad needs to go out today, or I need to have an urgent meeting with my team, or I need to work on this strategy right now. But such a decision hasn't brought me as many great results as I'd thought. Surprisingly, I am able to achieve more when I work out compared to when I don't. Taking just an hour off from your busy schedule and working on your own health can do wonders for you.

Exercise for Better Ideas

Your mind is the biggest tool for the growth of your business. But a mind needs so much to flourish and to work properly. Most importantly, it needs a healthy body where it can reside.

Your business can fail but if you have a strong mind, you can build another one. In contrast, if you are not physically and mentally strong, any kind of failure, even temporary ones can shake you badly.

Let's say that you prioritize your business over your health. One day you fall sick. As you haven't paid attention to your physical health, your body is going to take longer than normal to recover. In case you take a week to recover, you are going to lose almost seven days of productive work. One hour of exercise would have costed you only seven hours a week but a week-long sickness would cost you six times more than that.

As a business owner, your goal should also be to keep the downtime as low as you can and that becomes possible when you are able to fight off illnesses better than normal. For that, you will have to make your mind and body strong.

But that's not it.

Exercise makes you more productive. According to renowned psychiatrist John J. Ratey, M.D., exercise can fight memory loss, sharpen your intellect and can help you function better than ever. His research shows the extraordinary effects of breaking a sweat and the mind-body connection.[33]

Lifestyle Influences Your Health

Your lifestyle influences your health a lot. Sitting in front of a computer for so long and working on your business idea can harm your body. But you can bring changes in your life by just adopting a healthy lifestyle. Don't spend your entire day sitting on a couch. Take as many breaks as you can. Walk whenever you can.

Go to the gym or workout at your home. Don't skip it. Athletes are not the only ones who are in dire need of exercising, entrepreneurs equally are. I'm not asking you to break any records in weightlifting, biking or something else. If you can, then that's amazing. But all I'm asking you to do is to make sure your body doesn't get rusted because of your inactive lifestyle.

A rusted body will lead to a rusted mind and a rusted mind will not generate very effective ideas.

Another thing that good health can do for you is can save you from unexpected and unwanted burnouts. Many times, what happens when you're working on your business non-stop without seeing much results, is that you eventually lose all your energy, feel inactive, tired and unmotivated. At a stage like that, it is possible that you can accept it as an end to your entrepreneurial journey. But as Napoleon Hill said that your temporary failures should not turn into your permanent defeats. And when you are demotivated, chances are high that you can mistake your temporary failures as your permanent ones.

Above all, don't forget to sleep for normal hours. It has been studied that a good night sleep not just makes you clear-headed so you can make better decisions, but it also makes you more creative.[34]

You don't have to wake up at 4am just because a few CEO's are doing that. Different people are creative at different times of the day. To illustrate I am the most productive in the morning, my best friend in the night, and my husband during daytime. And it's totally okay. We all don't have to follow the same routine. Find your time when you're the most productive and creative and build your routine around it.

And don't compromise with your sleep. Sleep needs to make you feel refreshed. If you wake up and still feel tired, then you're not getting enough sleep or you're not following a healthy lifestyle. Either way, you need to bring some changes in your lifestyle.

Food and Nutrition to Keep You Creative

I am not a nutritionist, I'm just a marketer and a business owner. But I know that food and nutrition effects your mind a lot. My work is mainly dependent on building strategies which I'm able to come up with because I feed my mind with the kind of nutrition it needs to function.

In addition to keeping your mind active, proper nutrition can also help you fight depression. Sounds strange but it is true. Poor food choices can negatively affect the severity and duration of depression.[35] A healthy body and a healthy mind can keep the depression away. One of the main pieces of advice given to depressed people is to start moving and exercising!

Even though you are time-starved, you don't have to live on unhealthy junk food just because they are fast and can save you a lot of time. You need to set your priorities straight.

First it is you, and then it's your business. You don't have to spend your entire day cooking and exercising. But one hour of exercise every day with the introduction of healthy food options in your diet is all you need.

A Healthy Mind - Your Biggest Business Asset

72% of entrepreneurs have mental health issues.[36] That's a very big number! And you have to work from your side to make sure you don't fall in this category. This can only happen if you work on your mental health.

A business owner needs to be mentally stable and strong. A healthy mind will help you in fighting off any competition re-lated issues, legal issues, financial issues, team issues and even your personal issues. In addition, a strong mind will boost your self-confidence and will make you a better leader. Most import-antly, a healthy mind will train you in facing your adversity like a champ.

Next time when there's an unexpected roadblock in your project, you won't just stress out, or feel demotivated, but you will find a way out of it very easily.

Meditation for a Strong Mind

According to a study, entrepreneurs are more likely to report a lifetime of depression (thirty percent), atten-tion hyperactivity deficit disorder (twenty-nine percent), bipolar spectrum disorder (twelve percent) and substance abuse (eleven percent).[37]

If your mind is not strong enough to face the challenges that a business may bring, it's very easy to fall in the clutches of despair and anxiety. Meditation can help you take your mental health into your own hands.

Meditation can actually save your business. It might seem unbelievable, but it is true. When you live in the present moment, you're able to achieve higher productivity and use your day fully. Your ability to focus on a problem and figure out the solution increases tenfold. Meditation teaches us to quiet down every distraction, disturbance and just concentrate on the most important thing in the present moment. This awareness brings better solutions to problems.

One study has found out that meditation improves both verbal and non-verbal reasoning.[38] You are able to better analyze the information at hand for better decisions. You will also be able to grasp things faster and better. Above all, you won't drown in the flood of information and won't lose your ability to process all of that in a short time span. Meditation improves your memory, concentration and learning power.

Another study states that meditation improves the quality of sleep.[39] The better sleep you get, the more clear-headed you'll be to face your day-today issues. When you sleep better, your stress level decreases.

Ultimately, you gain better control of your emotions which gives you the power of improved and uninfluenced emotional decision making. Because when you get emotional when making a decision, you end up making decisions that match your emotional needs of that moment rather than your business needs. That's why emotional stability becomes very important for your entrepreneurial journey. You don't want to make a decision when you are sad or when you're overjoyed. Your emotions need to be in control when the time comes for decision making. If you want to learn to master your emotions, meditation becomes a must.

Meditation also keeps you cheerful and who couldn't use

more happiness in their lives? A positive mood will increase your energy level which will cause you to be excited and motivated to work on your business. One of the best ways that meditation can make you feel is more optimistic, and you can definitely benefit from that.

Positive Thinking for Self-Affirmations

There are so many people who will tell you that you can't do this, but you have to make sure that your voice isn't going to be one of them. It's not easy to be positive all the time. When everybody raises questions about your business, there is a chance that even you will end up questioning the future of your business.

"Will my business become successful? Is it going to make money? What if it fails? What will all the people around me say?" You can't let these thoughts enter your head. To fight such occasional negative thoughts which can turn regular even, you need to befriend positive thinking. If you think you have any kind of doubts and negativity regarding yourself or your capabilities to make your business profitable, then you have to get rid of these thoughts. The main thing that you have to focus on is that you're going to make your dream business come true and not make any of the 17 mistakes I have talked about in this book.

Start training your brain to think about your success. A little positive affirmation can't harm anyone. Affirmations do not create magic, but they are good to remind yourself that you're doing great, and it can create a positive mindset.

Here's what you have to do. Take a few minutes out of your schedule every now and then and remind yourself why you can achieve your goals. Make sure that your brain is getting enough training in seeing you and your business as a success and as a winner and not as a failure. This is also going to help you in breaking any negative thought cycle and getting rid of any self-limiting doubts that you have.

Another thing that you can do is practice gratefulness. Gratefulness helps us in focusing on the positive things in our lives rather than on the negative ones. This helps our brain in becoming more positive.

Practicing this gratefulness will make you a better problem solver. You won't spend your time criticizing yourself or engaging in negative thoughts. When you're optimistic, positive and cheerful, you attract similar things. No, I'm not talking magic here. I'm just telling you how the brain works. The brain is very interesting.

Henry Ford said, "If you think you can or can't do it, you're right in both cases."

If that's how the brain works, then why not start focusing on cans and not on the cant's? Let's give our 100% to our business this way nothing can stop success from coming to us.

You don't have to run away from your physical and mental health issues, but you have to work on them. If you see any signs of bad health, seek help. Don't worry about what people will think or if it's going to hurt your image of being a strong business leader.

There is no stigma or taboo attached to any of these words. On the other hand, **taking care of your physical and mental health is a sign of strength.** It shows that you are able to identify the problem on time and work on it. Isn't that what a business owner does?

Productivity is very important, and for that your well-being is very important. It's time for you to become more motivated, creative and goal-oriented, and you start that journey by taking care of yourself.

References

33. http://www.johnratey.com/
34. https://www.sciencedaily.com/releases/2007/05/070501075246.htm
35. https://www.ncbi.nlm.nih.gov/pmc/articles/PMC2738337/
36.https://www.startupgrind.com/blog/genius-in-madness-72-of-entrepreneurs-affected-by-mental-health-conditions/
37.https://michaelafreemanmd.com/Research_files/Are%20Entrepreneurs%20Touched%20with%20Fire%20(pre-pub%20n)%204-17-15.pdf
38. http://www.sciencedirect.com/science/article/pii/S1053810010000681
39. http://link.springer.com/article/10.1207/s15327558ijbm1204_9

CHAPTER 17

Not Investing in Yourself

"The important thing is not to stop questioning; curiosity has its own reason for existing." – Albert Einstein

The Story of Being Non-Curious

Have you ever met business owners who are still conducting their businesses the old way and it makes you wonder which era are they even living in?

These are the business owners who have stopped moving with time and stopped being curious about the new things.

I have a similar story to share with you of Mr. Carlos Garcia whose business failed because he had stopped investing in himself. Mr. Garcia ran his packaging company for over thirty years. Everything went smoothly until now when business process started turning digital. Instead of learning why everyone is going digital, he kept sticking to his old ways of doing things even more. He has done his business non-digitally for over thirty years and now he has no desire to change in his mid-sixties.

This mindset is nothing new and happens with all of us. Many of us are stuck in the 60s while many others are in the 90s. Some of us still don't understand the concept of torn jeans, lip syncing on TikTok, or the concept of digitally created music. In our personal lives, we can live in whichever decade we want to but unfortunately, the business line is not very accommodating. You can dress up like an 80s girl and listen to 80s music, but you can't run your business like you did in the 80s. You have to move ahead with time.

People from earlier generations don't understand the purpose of Instagram but they love Facebook, people before those generations don't even see any point in being on social media and people from my generation don't see any point of being on TikTok.

This viewpoint can be applied to so many other areas. Have you ever asked yourself what kind of business is this new generation into? In a way, we are trying to stick to something from our own time and are not willing to adapt to new changes. We can't say that in our times we used to do work this way, so we are going to continue doing it the same way.

Stagnation is the fall of a business.

When you become stagnant and aren't improving by the day, you are only moving toward your failure. The same happened with Mr. Garcia. He didn't change his ways of doing business when things started changing around him. He had always treated digital ways as irrelevant for his business because his business was B2B, or as per him was dependent on word-of-mouth marketing and not digital marketing, or some other excuse. He became stagnant, his knowledge became rusted, he didn't let new learning enter his mind and make him see the new, better and more efficient ways of doing the same thing.

His company was then challenged by other companies where

people were hungry for learning and were figuring out new ways to capture the industry. Later he decided to go digital, but it was too late.

Soon, his company was wiped off the market. He could have saved his company, had only he invested in himself, never stopped learning more about his business and how the business processes are evolving with time.

Never Stop Learning

We can never reach a stage where we can say, "I know everything, and I have nothing more left to learn." There is always something more that you can learn about your industry, your business, your product or yourself. It can be as simple as how to appreciate your employees more or it can be a little complex as to how to digitally transform your entire business. You can even learn how to do the same thing in a different way, so it saves time. There is no shortage of the things that you can learn to get better.

Our growth stops when overconfidence of being the best takes over.

You have to surround yourself with people who make you realize that there is so much that you don't know yet. **If you're the smartest person in a crowd, then either increase the size of that crowd or become a part of another crowd.** Keep doing it until you no longer remain the smartest person, until your ideas become challenged by others, and until you're forced to rethink that this is an interesting concept and I am going to learn more about it.

Here are a few other things that you can do:

- Turn Your Ideas into Action
  Ideas! Visions!

These are all fancy words and non-existent things until they are acted upon. You have to turn your vision into an action because otherwise it's mere useless. If the ideas are not exposed to other people in the world, those ideas don't do us any good. Imagine if Edison had kept his electricity idea to himself, and if Newton didn't want to do anything after his profound realization when an apple hit his head. This world would have been a different place!

An idea gains value when you take action to bring it to life. So, the next time if you have any interesting thoughts, any idea, or just an inkling, work toward it. See if this can be the next big thing, if this is something that can bring the change.

- ## Learn from Your Mistakes

When we fail, we get so disappointed, we lose our energy, all the excitement and motivation to work and succeed. So, we crawl back into our cocoon without realizing that we could have turned into a butterfly very soon if we hadn't accepted one small mistake as our failure.

Failures are a part of our lives, that too a very important part. It's only when we fail that we try to figure out a new and improved way that nobody has ever thought of.

Failures bring transformations in our society, in our lives and in the world.

Failures are just disguised teachings. I've started many businesses that have failed but I don't consider it a part of my life that I don't want to think about. As it's only because of all those failures that I have gained so many insights that I've utilized as a stepping-stone for my future successful businesses. I see many people making the same mistake that I did and that's why I thought of writing this book.

Failures are not scary! Failures are nothing to be scared of! They are to be embraced! Every failure shows that you're getting closer and closer to something big.

Meet your failure as the bigger person, learn the lesson, make changes in your plan and work again.

Use Your Time Efficiently

Getting distracted is nothing but human. Having unfaltering determination for your business to succeed is a very tough thing. I receive so many calls from my clients each month with a totally new business idea, just because they are losing patience with their main business idea.

Not just that, I have also seen many other people who think of starting an ecommerce business of clothing, but suddenly start talking about opening up a restaurant or a yoga center because they think the latter will have less competition.

As you may notice, none of these ideas are connected! An ecommerce business, a restaurant or a yoga studio – they're like apples, oranges and bananas we are talking about. How a person who was once passionate about fashion ecommerce is thinking about opening a restaurant is very confusing. The human mind keeps traveling from one idea to another as it becomes impatient. But you have to make sure that you don't get distracted - not by different business ideas, nor by any other thing.

With this in mind, there's no need to spend extra time in unnecessary decoration of your office, perfecting your website or your social media channels. When we are distracted, we do things like that. I myself have spent countless hours improving websites of my old businesses before realizing that perfection can't be achieved.

You will be distracted, but you have to stick to your strategy. Work as per your strategy, don't roam here and there.

- ## Grow with Your Business

   We are always working hard to grow our business but what we forget in this entire process is our own entire growth.

   Both our personal and business growth is oddly interconnected.

   When we grow, we come up with better ideas and solutions which help us in doing our business in more enhanced and productive ways.

   So, **don't just modernize and digitize your business, but also yourself.**

   Transform yourself into the most efficient tool and most performing asset of your business. If there is new technology out there that can benefit your business, take a course on it, if you think you can benefit from a calm mind, invest in some meditation courses. Try to be still for two minutes before making strong decisions.

   The opportunities to grow are endless and so are your options.

- ## Learn to Say No

   This is one of the principal things you have to learn if you are working on your business growth. Learning to say no! It seems very easy as if you never have to remind yourself of this, but it is very tough. You have to make yourself strong to say no to anything which interferes with your work.

   You have to start prioritizing your tasks and start saying no to things that can wait. Do you want to watch that movie right now or prepare your business plan as your meeting with the investors is coming very soon? No to movies and yes to business planning. Do not feed your procrasdemon - a demon that lives inside you that makes you procrastinate.

Do you want to organize your emails and clean up your laptop or do you want to finish the marketing research project so the social media ads can at least start? You know where to say no.

In no way am I promoting that you should start prioritizing your professional life over your personal life. We have to keep the two things in perfect balance but what I am suggesting is that when you are working on a new business or working from home during a pandemic, it's easy to get distracted by many unnecessary activities and thoughts.

I am not saying never watch that movie you were planning to. All I'm saying is watch it after you finish your high priority tasks like preparing your business plan. Similarly, I am not terming organizing your emails as a bad task as it's a good thing which helps you find the right information at the right time. What I'm implying here is that it shouldn't be prioritized over other high priority tasks. It can definitely wait until you finish other important tasks from your to-do list.

- ## Be Open to New Ideas
  Change is an inseparable part of your business. For this reason, you will need to replace your old ways of thinking. This becomes possible when you are flexible, when you know that others can be right as well and can have equally great ideas and you are willing to listen to them and if need be, even shed your old ideas and adapt to theirs.

Never Give Up

On the path of entrepreneurship, mistakes are unavoidable. Temporary mistakes should never turn into your permanent failure. Every time there is a mistake, learn from it, change the plan and keep moving forward.

The hush-hush secret of building a successful business is hidden in the mindset of never giving up.

Turn any obstacles into new learning, threats into opportunities and keep moving. Keep taking one step at a time but don't stop. Simple things like moving one foot ahead of the other on repeat can ultimately bring you closer to your goals.

You can bring about change in your life right now by not doing the following:

- ## Self-Doubt

  Self-doubt leads to giving up. If you know you have a good idea, if you have done the necessary research for it, then you have to keep any kind of doubt away from entering your mind. You don't have to think it is time to let it go but you have to think how you're going to make your idea possible.

  I am a big proponent of positive thinking. The kind of thoughts you have will attract the same kinds of things. If you believe you can do it, you will figure out a way of doing it. If you think you want to give up, then you will definitely find a good enough excuse to convince yourself to give up.

  This is something that we notice a lot among artists. Creativity and sensitivity go hand in hand. This explains why most of the artists are very sensitive souls. Pouring their emotions out in the form of their art makes them vulnerable and even doubt their own work. The fear of facing criticism and ridicule creeps in and in the end, the world loses some of the most amazing art. So, if you're an artist, please don't let anything stop you from creating and sharing your art. This world can benefit from your work quite a lot.

● Lack of Motivation

Even if you are working on your own dream idea, losing motivation with time is very much possible. When you are working for a few years, maybe even for a few months without seeing any results, it gets very tough to keep that entrepreneur enthusiasm alive.

Not just the motivation of our employees, we have to make sure to keep even our own motivation up at all times. There are so many different ways to keep the well of motivation in you always full.

For example, you can keep some notes next to you to remind you what you're working on and why you started working on this idea in the very first place. Look at that note after waking up, before going to bed and all those times you lose motivation, and let your body absorb those words.

There are two kinds of people - one who can motivate themselves and the one who needs somebody else to motivate them. If you're in the first category, every day having some kind of reminder of your ultimate goal can help you stay energetic and excited about your venture.

However, if you're the one who needs some kind of external motivation, then make sure to keep one of your loved ones involved in your project as well. This loved one will help in bringing your spirits up when you feel down. It can be any one of your family members, your partner, or your spiritual guru.

● Not Believing in Your Own Product

The best advice I can give you is to never stop believing in your product. When you believe in your product, others will as well. When you doubt your product, others will doubt it ten times more than you. If others start doubting your product, they will never buy it from you. If they won't buy it, your product will fail.

When we sell our idea, our product or any kind of service, we also sell the feelings and emotions we have that are associated with that. When we sell a product that we trust ourselves, we sell the same feelings of trust and belief for that product to the buyer. The buyer feels more content after their purchase. Soon, that buyer transfers that feeling of trust in other people. When many people besides yourself start believing in your product, you pave the way of success for yourself.

The easiest way of making others believe in you is by believing in yourself. It's as simple as this if you think you can't do this, how can you believe that others will think that you can do this. After all, you know yourself better than others do.

- ## Not Overcoming Your Fear of Business Failure
  Success and failure are a part of a business life. Successful businesses can fail and failing businesses can succeed. What is more important than success and failure is that you continue trying. When you continue working on your business idea without any fear of business failure, you are able to figure out various ways of succeeding.

- ## Letting Your Negative Thoughts Determine Your Success
  Thoughts are very important. What you put in your mind, is going to be what you put out in your day to day life. If you

think you can never succeed, then it's the same belief you're going to put into your business.

Our thoughts are very powerful. Not only do they transform us internally, but they also transform the external world around us. Don't let these thoughts be any kind of garbage because garbage in means garbage out. Let these thoughts be pillars of strength and support, and you will find yourself surrounded with the same. And trust me you're going to need a ton of that when you're working on your business idea.

Giving Up Too Early

Persistence is very important. Without persistence, we give up so early even before we are ready. Giving up is bad but giving up early is even worse because in the second case, we haven't even tried enough. We've accepted our defeat even before we even played all of our cards.

Great things take time. Your business idea is one of those things. If it's taking time, it means your idea is trying to bring a big societal and cultural change. These changes don't happen so fast. We don't just start driving cars from riding horses or shopping online instead of going to stores; all these changes have taken a lot of time.

There is a direct correlation between your marketing and advertising budget and the time required to reach your goals. If your budget is low, you might need more than the standard time to reach your goal and if your budget is bigger, you might be able to cover that journey faster. But in both the cases, there is no need to quit.

In the first case, you should accept that it's going to take a few years before you see any outcome. It can even take three to seven years. I know many entrepreneurs who have been working on their idea for more than five years. It's taking time but it doesn't imply that their product is not good.

In the second case, you will be required to spend a little extra, but a little investment doesn't do any harm. Investments are how Warren Buffet has made over $85.6 billion.

The Fairy of Overnight Success

There is no such thing as overnight success. Everything takes time. As Malcolm Gladwell explored in his book, *Outlier*, all the people we find very successful like Bill Gates, The Beatles and many others actually have been working for quite a long time before they'd hit their overnight success. In his terms, it took them at least 10,00 hours of hard work before they became experts or had overnight success.

Adrien Brody, a popular American actor once said, "My dad told me, 'It takes fifteen years to be an overnight success,' and it took me seventeen and a half years."

There are so many insights hidden in those words by Adrien Brody. Many business owners have told me how their business is going to be a million-dollar business by next year, but it never happened. As it's a big dream and big dreams take a lot of effort, hard work and time before they reach the stage of success.

Don't fall for the idea of overnight success. You can't become a successful blogger in a month. Honestly, not even in a year. In fact, not even in three years. Ask all the big bloggers how much time it took before they had started earning huge amounts. I am sure the answer will surprise you. Most of them have been in industry for over ten years.

There can be overnight failure but success and believing in overnight success will only bring you closer to overnight failure.

In the end, don't give up unless and until you are out of all your cards or ideas. However, if you never want to run out of ideas, you should start investing in yourself. This helps your brain in generating better ideas.

Make sure that every day you're learning something new, that every day you are working on creating your version 2.0. Learning doesn't end when you graduate but learning only starts at that time. If you think you have done your undergrad and grad, so you're good, then I am afraid to tell but you are highly mistaken. You still have a lot to learn.

When running a business, you are going to handle so many roles, and every role will require a lot of training. So, my question to you is what did you learn today? Are you a better version of yourself than you were yesterday?

About the Author

Pooja Agnihotri is the Chief Marketing Officer of Bizadmark based in New York.

Her effective value-driven marketing strategies with a focus on building profitable customer relationships have helped over 100 businesses including Fortune 500 companies grow and become profitable.

She has spent more than a decade building meaningful and powerful connections between customers and businesses to drive sustainable business growth for brands. She is a strong advocate of purpose-driven marketing and the humanization of brands that have led to the improvement in how brands interact with customers and communities across North America, Europe, Australia, and Asia.

She is passionate about the future and how technology, data, and creativity can be used in marketing to make the world a better place not just for brands but also for our planet. You can contact her at pooja@bizadmark.com.

Made in the USA
Middletown, DE
12 May 2022